Acclaim for *Cultiva~* ~

"This is one of the most important and profound books of our time. In luminous prose, the great visionary activist James O'Dea communicates the ideals and practices of peace in ways that summon a spiritual and social evolution. At once both tough and tender, this masterpiece is the finest map I know to the transformation of self and civilization. If you read only one book this year, this is it!"

—**Jean Houston,** founder of the field of Social Artistry

"This marvelous book has the potential to grow peacebuilding to the point that every school, every business, and every community incorporates these principles. James O'Dea's life experience and skillful writing make peacebuilding personal and accessible. He shows us that 'cultivating peace' is not just what UN diplomats or professional mediators do. It's a vital part of each of our lives."

—**Mark Gerzon,** best-selling author of
Leading Through Conflict and *Global Citizens*

"O'Dea liberates our imagination about peace; his insights enrich the field of conflict transformation."

—**Abdul Aziz Said,** Professor of International Relations,
American University, and founder, International Peace
and Conflict Resolution Program

"This brilliant manifesto weaves science, spirituality, and social healing into a practical peace roadmap for us all."

—**Deepak Chopra**, author of *Peace Is the Way*

"The peace movement, and what Kenneth Boulding called the much broader 'movement toward peace' in human consciousness, has long been fragmented, without a compelling and unifying narrative—and therefore is much less effective as a cause than is implied by the power of the truths it contains. James O'Dea's book is an important contribution toward the articulation of that narrative, especially bringing out the many inner components of peacebuilding—the only place from which peace can really come."

—**Professor Michael Nagler,** cofounder of the Peace and Conflict
Studies Program at UC Berkeley, founder of the Metta Center
for Nonviolence, and author of *The Search for a Nonviolent Future*

"James O'Dea is a modern-day prophet who has journeyed further than any-one I know in search of the ways of peace. He is both a consummate scholar and an unwavering activist whose lifework has been in service of a peaceful world. In his brilliant new book, *Cultivating Peace*, he tells the real and deep truth about what peace really is and what it takes to bring it forth in today's troubled world. This book is O'Dea's long-awaited magnum opus, a wise and unprecedented guide to the social healing that our world urgently needs now."

—**Lynne Twist**, author of *The Soul of Money* and
cofounder of the Pachamama Alliance

"This superbly written and seminal guide to peacemaking by the brilliant and visionary James O'Dea reveals a profound truth: peacemaking is a two-way, transformational process that begins in our own hearts. *Cultivating Peace* is so packed full of nuggets of wisdom for both self-transformation and spiritual activism that it should come with a warning: read this book only when you're prepared to heal yourself and everyone around you."

—**Lynne McTaggart,** international best-selling author
of *The Intention Experiment* and *The Bond*

"James O'Dea is indubitably one of the most evolved souls on this planet. He can advise others on how to become a global peace ambassador because he is one himself. The spread of his message worldwide is one of the key precondi-tions of creating a peaceful transformation worldwide—and in time."

—**Ervin Laszlo,** renowned systems theorist and
founder of Global Shift University

"Don't dismiss James O'Dea as a simple zealot for peace. Instead, he is a sophisticated ambassador for a new humanity and world system. *Cultivating Peace* is a wise and warmhearted book that is seasoned by years of firsthand experience in the reality of human conflict. O'Dea invites us to change our collective story, awaken to a global consciousness, and envision the great work of deep reconciliation as the foundation for a promising future."

—**Duane Elgin**, author of *Voluntary Simplicity*,
The Living Universe, and *Awakening Earth*

"James O'Dea penetrates to the soul level where the source of love lives. By recognizing and loving that universal essence of being within us, no matter who we are, he reveals and heals the violence. He provides us with a path that each of us can follow to heal ourselves and the world. I find that every moment I spend with him is precious and brings peace to my soul."

—**Barbara Marx Hubbard**, renowned evolutionary leader and
author of *Conscious Evolution* and *Birth 2012 and Beyond*

Cultivating Peace

Cultivating Peace

Becoming a 21st-Century Peace Ambassador

James O'Dea

Shift Books

PO Box 151117 • San Rafael, CA 94915
www.shiftmovement.com

Copyright © 2012
By James O'Dea

Cover design by Stevee Postman
Interior book design by Carla Green

Library of Congress Control Number: 2011943614

ISBN: 9780984840717

Cataloging-in-Publication Data:

O'Dea, James.
    Cultivating peace : becoming a 21st century peace ambassador /
    James O'Dea
    p. cm.
    Includes bibliographical references and index.
    LCCN 2011943614
    ISBN 9780984840717

    1. Conflict management. 2. Peace-building. 3. Peace. I. Title.

HM1126.O34 2012   303.6'9
                          QBI12-600077

First printing April 2012
Printed in the United States of America on recycled paper
9 8 7 6 5 4 3 2 1

To two ambassadors of peace:
Michael A. Singer and Abdul Aziz Said

Contents

Acknowledgments

I would like to begin with well-deserved recognition to Byron Belitsos, who has launched Shift Books in collaboration with the Shift Network. Byron is erudite, visionary, and passionate. The combination of these skills leads to exacting and masterful editing that any author who works with him is privileged to experience. I am also grateful for the Zen-like precision of Karen Seriguchi whose editing skills are without equal.

I also wish to acknowledge Stephen Dinan for his visionary leadership in founding the Shift Network and managing its growth so successfully. Stephen holds a vision of planetary transformation that is both audacious and coherent. I am grateful to be a part of the Shift Network's trailblazing journey. Some of the original material in this book comes from teaching a course for the Shift Network called The Path of the Peacemaker and from being the lead faculty of its sixteen-week-long Peace Ambassador Training, which has trained close to five hundred peace ambassadors in over thirty countries. The staff at the Shift Network who organize and skillfully steer these trainings are exceptional peacebuilders themselves. I would like to recognize the whole team, especially Emily Hine and Philip Hellmich.

To colleagues at Amnesty International, the Seva Foundation, and the Institute of Noetic Sciences who have nurtured my growth, I offer great thanks. Specifically, I owe a debt to Judith Thompson,

Belvie Rooks, Sequoyah Trueblood, and Molly Rowan Leach for our long journey through the world's wounding ways to the path of social healing.

Finally, there is a Sufi expression, "the best is hidden." That has largely been the case with the unfathomably beautiful souls who have guided my spiritual development—they have, in most cases, avoided the glare of the marketplace and the media. My teachers are like the jasmine whose flowers only release their fragrant secrets as the daytime's brilliant sunlight gives way to the evening's subtler shifts of light and energy. The only way to honor them is to breathe them in and experience peace.

Introduction

If you have a nose for what is in the wind, it will have sensed an exponential rise in people power across the planet. The world's people are making their needs and values known as never before. They are pouring into the streets and sometimes staying there until they are heard. They are exchanging ideas, giving support to systemic transformation, sharing organizing models, and getting to know each other at ever-accelerating rates of connectivity. A sleeping giant is awakening in the masses of humanity. It is conscious, and it is aware of its rights. And behold, this awakened giant, though not prone to violence, is decidedly averse to being dominated.

The year 2011 will be long remembered for the struggle of Arab peoples throughout the Middle East to end dictatorships. The Arab Spring is part of a planetary springtime that has included the emergence of the Occupy movement and unprecedented levels of street protest in dozens of countries. These blossoming movements are rising up in the face of fiercely adverse conditions. Springtime has its own kind of resilience.

The first crocus can raise its head even before the snow has departed. If you have a good eye for patterns, you will see these first crocuses everywhere, rising out of the hardened soil of a long planetary winter in which world wars, genocides, and ethnic and ideological violence claimed more than a hundred million lives in the preceding century.

The real promise in the flowering of all this movement is the first emergence of a planetary culture of peace.

Meanwhile, the peace movement itself is undergoing it own regenesis and transformation. It is shifting from being framed solely by its opposition to war and human rights violations to the systemic work of creating nonviolent cultures and just and sustainable societies. Peace can no longer be reduced to flags, banners, and protest movements. Peace is the source of health, well-being, skillful mediation, dialogue, conflict resolution, fruitful and productive relationships, empathy, compassion, social justice, genuine freedom, cultural diversity, true democracy, and enlightened local and global governance. Peace is so large and encompassing because it brings together inner security and global security. Peace links the inner life and the whole web of life with its requirements for sustainability and equity on a global scale. Finally we are looking at a map of peace that includes broad worldview reframing as well as changes in specific beliefs and behaviors and their enactment on a large scale.

An ambassador of peace is someone who recognizes the importance of transforming both inner blockages to peace and those blockages in external relations, cultures, and systems that prevent peace in the world. Peace ambassadors become skillful in learning the art, the practice, and the science of peace while cultivating peace within themselves. As fluently as they model and express peace, they learn to reflect and embody it.

Today's peace movement has a new imperative: to mirror the change it is looking for in the world and not to wait for others to deliver it. "Be the change" has become a central motif of the emerging peace movement because evolution now requires a transformation of inner consciousness matched with a capacity to reach measurable social goals and to master daunting political challenges. We have begun to see that we cannot address the problem of violent aggression without changing fundamental beliefs and addressing the cultural and structural underpinnings of violence.

As a result, a new map for the peace movement is also emerging, a map that goes much deeper within and much further out into whole-systems change, thus framing the problem far more widely than the former practice of merely opposing those who instigate wars or those who profit from arms sales. Psychology, spirituality, science, and systems theory are now at the table with law, political science, diplomacy, and other more established approaches to social change and political negotiation. What is emerging is a map of the whole that looks at the dynamic and interactive nature of the relationship between parts and whole, inner and outer. And finally, this new chart of the way to peace requires a greater mastery of subtlety and complexity. Peace is a complex equation far beyond who is right and who is wrong, who takes home the most money or who has the most stuff. Peace requires a subtle appreciation of cultural nuance and local conditions. We cannot get to peace without understanding the complex relationship between plurality and unity. This book is about that new map, its new requirements and the movement it heralds.

But the map is not the territory. *Cultivating Peace* takes the reader into the territory of peacebuilding and does not leave you at the door with simple "how to" formulas. You know when you are in the territory by the way it starts to stimulate a richness and fullness in your heart and mind and the way it stirs you to act. Peace has a sensorial and embodied aspect that gives you a direct experience of it. I invite you to think about peace in new ways and also to taste peace.

Each chapter begins with a presentation of new concepts, followed by a direct call to the reader to activate these new modalities. The chapter then concludes with a brief reflection oriented to specific ways to practice peacebuilding and to engage in the work of being an ambassador of peace.

You are invited to enter the consciousness that *Cultivating Peace* not only seeks to describe but also attempts to convey an experience of. The best way to allow it to work on you is to approach this book as a mixture of information and insight, prose and poetry, science and mysticism. You may get frustrated if you don't allow these contrasting tones and voices to work on you. There is much to be studied in this book, and some of it may be conceptually demanding. But there is more to be savored. It is part peace methodology, part medicine.

As human consciousness evolves, it is capable of holding greater complexity. A more advanced awareness can see the context in which certain polarities cannot see themselves because they lack perspective and because they are caught in a dance of opposites. This expanded consciousness is naturally more spacious and flexible because it can embrace a wider and more inclusive truth. It knows how truth has many gradations and flavors and can be both linear and nonlinear. When truth gets caught in a battle of facts, this wider consciousness asks us to explore the truth of our feelings and experiences as well. It honors both subjective truth and objective truth. It honors the many dimensions of truth. *Cultivating Peace* reminds us that the emerging peace ambassador, in his or her efforts at being an authentic representative of peace, will be called upon to represent the subtlety of an expanded truth process.

So, in this book you will not be bludgeoned by the sense that you have to get on board with a unidirectional truth. At the same time, you will see that authentic truth cannot be expressed in milquetoast metaphors. In fact, you will find that I attempt to communicate the truth passionately and clearly in this book. Yet, at the same time, rigor mortis of the truth occurs in the absence of a living, interactive dynamic between your truth and mine.

Cultivating Peace begins with not taking ourselves so seriously. The first chapter, "Peace Is the Real Game Changer," reminds us that a world without laughter would not be a safe or peaceful world. Fundamentalists are without fun. Conviviality defines peace more than moral rectitude. Social cohesion is fostered by relational maturity and the ability to feel empathy for others even when they are being obnoxious or making fools of themselves. For example, visualize the face of the Dalai Lama beaming impish good humor and serene smiles that draw from a rich source of compassion and nonviolence. He is spiritual *and* political, meditative *and* engaged. No one could accuse him of not having fun. Yet the reasons he is a courageous and effective Nobel Peace Prize leader are obvious only when his lightness of being is understood. Laughter and relational maturity are crucial, but peace is the game changer. Contemporary science tells us we are designed for peace and that our health and longevity depend on it. In fact, our survival as a species requires that we end our investments in war and direct our attention toward solving our many looming challenges. The worldviews that have promoted excessive competition, environmental degradation, increased social inequity, religious bigotry, and perhaps widespread systemic collapse are clearly not adequate to the optimal evolution of our species. Chapter 1 also looks at how our evolutionary story is being changed by emerging worldviews and a transformation of belief.

Chapter 2, "Peace and Freedom from the Inside Out," explores worldview formation more deeply, specifically the all-important process of identification in the structuring of belief. I contrast moral maps, belief systems, and psychological perspectives. This chapter also explores how the emerging peace ambassador learns to synchronize the inner and outer.

Chapter 3, "Expanding Your Comfort Zone," contrasts rights and responsibilities and draws from the luminous vision of the Earth Charter in this regard. I explore the delicate balance between stretching to be more inclusive and finding comfort in your value system. Readers will also discover why peacemakers should be comfortable with conflict.

Chapter 4, "Ending the Transmission of Wounds," looks at how to interrupt the transmission of wounds from generation to generation precisely because their persistence is so disruptive to whole-system health and because the problem of passing on intergenerational trauma is so often overlooked. We have made great progress in recognizing how our personal beliefs and prior wounding affect personal health. Psychiatry helps us deal with personal trauma, but we are only just beginning to learn how to apply such knowledge at the societal level. We are beginning to see how truth, reconciliation, and forgiveness are essential components of collective healing strategies that also include engaged dialogic practice. When the inherited trauma of history is submerged in a collective wound, it rises again and again to subvert peace. This chapter reminds us that this need not be so and shares in depth the contemporary skills of the peacebuilder and social healer that can be applied to heal the past.

Nature gave us only one mouth, but two eyes and two ears. Listening is one of the defining skills of peaceful human development, and it is by no means passive. In fact, it may be one of the most proactive things we can do. Chapter 5, "Peaceful Communication: Engaged Listening," offers a detailed review of types of listening. It covers transactional, cognitive process, postural, inquiry, heart-centered, and integral listening stances. We need to teach the dimensions of listening just as we teach good articulation and the nuances of the spoken word.

Let it be said that we became the listening planet. If others ever land from some distant part of the universe, let them be greeted not with missiles but with attention, awe, and interest. But we really don't need to fantasize about visitors from distant worlds, for it seems we have created so many kinds of otherness here in our own world. Some forms of otherness represent ignorance and prejudice that can be dissolved through skillful listening.

Chapter 6, "Peaceful Communication: Facts, Experience, and Truth," is central to understanding how we can move from purely legalistic frameworks of truth recovery to constructs that validate the truth of people's experience. Numerous historical truth commissions have served the cause of peace instead of retaliatory violence and cyclical vengeance. The most widely discussed has been the South African Truth and Reconciliation Commission, which established a new benchmark for peaceful resolution of historical enmity.

Chapter 7, "Peaceful Communication and Energy Mastery," describes how we can learn to process energy for peaceful encounters with each other. It looks at the subject of bullying and outlines effective strategies for dealing with physical bullies, emotional bullies, and intellectual bullies. It also reviews different approaches to energy processing, by contrasting the energy bouncer, the energy sponge, the energy zapper, and the peaceful energy transformer.

Cultivating Peace provides three chapters on peaceful communication because where possible we must learn how to skillfully engage the other. None of us has a magic wand to transform versions of the other who seeks to trample on our values, suffocate our freedom, or breed exploitation and injustice. This book is no such magic wand. What lies ahead for humanity is fiercely challenging, and we will evolve only as our capacity to communicate peacefully evolves.

Chapter 8, "Achieving Peace through Creativity and Dialogue," deals with the opportunities available to peace activists through different modes of dialogue, inquiry, and structured conversation. Against all odds we must learn to dialogue, or die. In a whole-systems framework we are all connected; we are all implicated. None of us is without ego, but harm comes only when we surrender to it. This is no simple story of others' villainy versus our virtue. But one thing is clear: if we would learn how to dialogue deeply with others, the story would change. If we were to learn that listening to each other was the key to opening each other's hearts, we would listen until there was peace on earth. For listening is the precursor to sharing truth in truly meaningful exchange. Peacemakers as far back as our ancient ancestors have developed peace circles and deep sharing processes, and modern peace practitioners have learned to hone these tools as precision implements.

Chapter 9, "Peace Work and Whole-Systems Shift," provides an accessible view of the territory of systemic transformation and peace work in the context of complex adaptive systems. A detailed commentary is provided on a set of "simple rules" used for addressing complex systems. Deep in the weave of *Cultivating Peace* is the invitation to explore wholeness. To be an ambassador of peace, you cannot be a partisan of the part; you are called to be a representative of holistic thinking and emotional and social intelligence. Creating a culture of peace is a whole-systems challenge. For example, we are now witnessing the planetwide devastation that results from thinking of the economy and ecology as separate systems. Sustainability is, therefore, a peace issue; even the US military recognizes that armed conflicts may erupt as a result of resource scarcities and climate change. We also see the appalling societal problems that result from divorcing the realms of psychology, healing, and justice. By punishing when we could restore and heal, we seed more violence and criminality.

The final chapter names what it describes: "The 21st-Century Peace Ambassador as Evolutionary Leader." It covers a detailed list of the strengths and capacities of an evolved peace leader. In a time of upheaval such as we are now witnessing on planet Earth, unprecedented opportunities arise for creativity and new leadership. As the Dalai Lama reminds us, "It is not enough to be compassionate; one must act." The new-paradigm leader is not some amazingly charismatic character hewn of heroic qualities almost unattainable by the average person: the emerging peace leader is you! Throughout this book, I invite you to join me in playing your own decisive part in the story of our collective transformation. Without you, there is no new peace movement. Without our collective voice, there may be leaders, but there will be no surge in shared leadership and no exponential shift in collective behavior. Without you, there is no collective audacity to create the tipping point in human evolution. Peace is a story of mobilization. But the objective of the mobilization has changed: we are no longer storming the gates demanding peace and justice. The new peace movement has scaled the walls of everything that can hold us back, including our own beliefs, and we have entered the territory of enmity and exploitation to transform it from the inside out. But we are not zealots of peace; we are the ambassadors of a new humanity.

I have not included a discussion of personal inner-peace practice work in this book because so much has been written about it and because many cultures, religions, and spiritual traditions approach practice of this nature in contrasting ways. Rather, I assume that readers of *Cultivating Peace* are in alignment with its integral approach: again, the central interest and teaching of the book is in demonstrating how the inner and the outer are connected in the work of peacebuilding in the broadest sense. Once we understand that, we see how peace work is the great work that connects all disconnection and separation. In light of this principle, we as peace workers discover that sometimes we need to step back to do rigorous inner work, while at other times we need to summon our courage to step out to play our part in healing a conflicted world. But mostly, we need to synchronize inner and outer with a new level of skillfulness and integrity. That state of synchronization is, I believe, the elixir of peace. It is my deepest wish that each one of us gets to drink of it deeply.

Chapter 1

~

Peace Is the Real Game Changer

Traditionally, we think of peace as a serious matter. When people demand peace, it is usually because their lives have become a hell because of war and terror. We see the expressions on their faces: agony, despair, anger, humiliation, and the loss of innocence. We have become all too familiar with the deep wounding of our veterans both physically and mentally: blown-off limbs, broken families, addiction, post-traumatic stress disorder, and elevated suicide rates. Even in the faces of those who protest war, we see the tightened contours of moral outrage and frustration at our human inability to settle differences without resorting to horrifying levels of violence.

I was very angry for a long time. I worked for Amnesty International for a decade, serving as the director of its Washington, DC, office. In those days, I believed that I had to pump up an adrenaline fury to fight the monstrous acts of governments that went to any extreme to silence their own people. We saved many, many lives and rescued people from obscene cruelty and torture, and that was no light achievement. In time, I came to learn that too much seriousness is deadly. We hugged a lot, laughed a lot, and even became highly inventive in playing elaborate jokes on one another.

Now, I don't intend to entertain you with black humor. Nor do I seek to cheer you up with a series of false positives designed to make you feel good or to spirit you away from contemplating the vile truth of human brutality. There will be time for tears, for honorable tears, and for opening the heart's core to the suffering of humanity; indeed, as we will see, it is only through understanding our wounding that we can cultivate healing. But for an important reason, I choose to begin this book by sounding a different note.

You see, it is hyperfanatical seriousness that gets us into trouble in the first place. Rage just isn't funny, is it? Any kind of overbearing behavior—be it self-righteousness, bigotry, aggression, condemnation, arrogance, or finger-pointing—is an interruption of the body's circuitry of love, joy, and play. It is the prologue, and the trigger, to deeper hostility and violence.

Not surprisingly, when we cultivate love and joyful service, we live longer, healthier, and happier lives. We don't need science to tell us this, but plenty of research backs it up.[1] I learned this in my role as president of the Institute of Noetic Sciences, where I had daily access to the world's best research on consciousness studies and mind-body medicine. The other side of the coin is equally obvious: stay continuously angry, and you will die younger. Whether or not we do violence to others, we do violence to ourselves when we fail to build networks of harmonious relationships in our lives and when we constrict our hearts around old resentments or fail to forgive or to move on.

Let's face it: people who instigate violence are uptight. In fact, they are constantly cooking a biochemical brew in their bodies that is toxic at every level—physically, emotionally, psychologically, and spiritually. They shut down the body's exquisite ease, delight, and pleasure signals and replace them with hypervigilance and stress alerts. They develop serious authority fixations because the only relief they get is through dominating others, pushing people around, or by themselves submitting to the safe orderliness of a rigid hierarchy.

When humor enters into this somber mix, it can be hijacked to become sarcasm or caricatures that are demeaning to others. The worst kind of racial and ethnic humor often shows up when threatened people are trying to reinforce their own in-group ties. In such contexts, jokes can have a strange way of revealing sadness, emptiness, hostility, and even viciousness. But true humor does not carry a poison pill. Think of the Dalai Lama, a great force for peace, constantly smiling and chuckling even as he faces enormous challenges on behalf of his people. See how his sweetness is a flowering of nonviolence, and you will understand what a contrast such a man of peace is to oppressive seriousness.

The absence of ordinary smiles and natural good humor can be a mark of ill will. Psychologists advise law enforcement and airport screeners to look out for the absence of natural smiling behaviors, because terrorists intent on killing others are usually pumping a biochemical brew that prevents them from smiling.

The lighter side of life has become the subject of much research and scientific inquiry. Humor and laughter are complex and difficult to fathom. But researchers universally agree that they are great for your health. Laughter releases endorphins and builds up our immune system. It removes the toxins of deep stress. For the mind in a state of stress, a moment of humor can set off a great game that starts off with the left brain's cognitive processing as it seeks to get the joke. The left brain alone, however, seems unable to work it out. So it passes the ball to the right brain, which synthesizes it and gets a gestalt of the whole picture. Then, when the humorous content is appreciated, the whole body joins in a chorus of emotional pleasure and sensorial appreciation.

Laughter is a signal that it is safe to drop our guard. It arouses our innate sense of play. It reawakens the primitive sense of freedom experienced by happy children. And there is quite a mystery in laughter, as it turns out: its power to bring people together to experience social communion in many instances defies rational explanation. Nevertheless, laughter has been the subject of serious research.

While we might quip that doing scientific research on this subject will not improve one's sense of humor, the research itself bears out that laughter and humor are only minimally linked. Something deeper than cleverness is at play. Studies also show that speakers are much more likely to laugh at their own jokes than their audiences are. I think this is probably especially true of politicians, who invariably seem to take themselves way too seriously. And here's an even more interesting fact: researchers have found that only 15 percent of the things people laughed at were humorous in any way. Strange indeed to find yourself dissecting jokes only to find that they are not funny!

But laughter is infectious. We laugh more in an atmosphere of laughter, just as we tend to be more fearful in an atmosphere of collective fear and threat. Laughter is essentially a communal activity; we are thirty times as likely to laugh with others as to laugh alone. Laughing is about the bubbling up of connection.

This effervescence of laughing and communing together and then our surrendering from there to the deeper joy of collaboration gives us a taste of the huge richness of this subject for peacebuilding. When we are plugged into the primal and unifying field of connection, for which laugher is an obvious but not exclusive door, our body and mind reward us with a cascading flow of inner delight that spreads to others.

Now, in light of these scientific discoveries, consider this implication for the peace ambassador: think of passionate purpose, play, high fun—indeed, the joys of working together to change a hugely depressing and dreary story—and you will be better able to take on the deadly serious merchants of war, oppression, scarcity, competition, and fear.

Peace is pleasurable, collective, and safe, but it needs the circuitry of connection to distribute its self-fulfilling reward. Humor, laughter, and play are among the best ways to make that connection as a peacebuilder.

Our bodies understand the rewards of peace

Sometimes a smile has the power to break the ice and begin a healing thaw. For good reason: the body prefers pleasure to pain. The body's role in supporting the ways of peace offers another layer for our consideration.

The body remembers rewards—just as it records pain and wounding. Our positive learning is connected to the production of the pleasure hormone dopamine. Video games, for example, are structured around dopamine hits: more rewards, more magic spells, more points if you keep winning. Once this positive hormonal reinforcement is better understood by ethical game designers, the element of overcoming risk and danger does not have to be linked only to bloody shoot-'em-up scenarios.

How we obtain our rewards and how they are marketed are always moral issues. Modern economies are oriented to rewards that are often accompanied by hidden costs and unsustainable inequities. Our bodies are constantly targeted to get them to consume things that will serve the profits of corporations more than our well-being. Part of our work is to de-condition our minds and bodies from artificial rewards and to learn to recognize the rewards that will come from living a more conscious lifestyle. Genuine peace will become possible when the rewards of health, wellness, and sustainability are the most attractive.

Peace is the ultimate reward to be experienced by the body because it is creatively self-renewing, but it occurs only if three conditions are present:

- if peace is experienced as dynamic, juicy, and empowering rather than as some kind of perpetually tamped-down flatland for righteous, serious, and supposedly virtuous people;
- if peace motivates our life's purpose by engaging our highest creativity and moral imagination; and
- if we manifest the passion, courage, emotional resilience, and deep generosity that peacebuilding requires.

Under these conditions, peace becomes the highest reward because it leads to serenity, acceptance, well-being, vitality, and a high quality of engagement with others. Peace is the masterpiece of our collective evolutionary striving precisely because it is not easy to acquire. It lures us to become our absolute best.

The central idea, again, is that tearing down the walls of separation is both deeply pleasurable and rewarding. There can be no peace and thus few rewards as long as we build our world behind walls that conceal fear, isolation, superiority, or distrust. But the kind of peace that stretches all the way from inner peace to international peace and security is capable of reversing the fortunes of a world that so often hideously inverts our highest values. That reversal begins in our individual lives when we feel *aroused* rather than obligated by the search for peace. And arousal is not fun if it does not connect with deep pleasure. In fact, it is meaningless if not directed toward reward.

The body collaborates with higher purpose to reward us with the biochemistry of pleasure in other ways as well. You have heard of the "helper's high" because it is true: philanthropy, altruism, and quality relationships are deeply rewarding. In fact, if we engage in these pro-human, pro-connective, and pro-community pursuits, research suggests that we will have better wellness indicators, more happiness, and more longevity. But the kind of pleasure I refer to is not accessible without moral commitment: it comes from surrendering to a vision or a call to service which then informs a life's work.

The rewards of peace are to be deeply appreciated: it feeds the heart, nourishes relationships, and awakens deep empathy and compassion. Once you understand the rewards of peace, nothing will prevent you from cultivating them or mobilizing all your energy to end the self-punishing belligerence of a world in which fanaticism has many guises.

Peace reframes the whole story

We can't just switch on peace. We can't just buy peace. Nor does peace result from an instant conversion. Peace is not collectively pursued at this time in human history because we habitually choose short-term rewards. Even as technology gives us the opportunity for vast collaboration, too many of us default in favor of narrow self-interest when using it. But such myopia will never achieve the sustained rewards of lasting peace. We have not collectively cracked the codes of peace because they interrupt the fundamental patterns of how we live, do business, and conduct social, political, and cultural life on earth.

Genuine peace represents a whole new order of being and an evolutionary reframing that entail the transformation of communication and cultural processes, new forms of participatory democracy, and the redesign of socioeconomic systems. This comprehensive vision of peace embodied in individuals and actualized in educational and political systems represents a new map of social reality. This map can seem hugely ambitious because its codes are about reframing the whole story from inside the psyche of humanity all the way out to its structures of organization and development. The emerging peace ambassador is invited to work toward wholesale systemic transformation without getting lost in naivety or in the pursuit of shortcuts to the rewards of peace. He or she must also avoid the pitfall of succumbing to the pervasive fatalism of those who are so heavily invested in maintaining the status quo that they give up hoping for real change.

Fatalism, in the form of the retrenched and vested interests of the power elites, takes the guise of being the voice of humanity's development, but scratch a little deeper, and you will find the cynical grim reaper more interested in profit than in genuine progress. Power brokers who show little concern for such things as community sustainability invariably speak in terms of *inevitabilities* that favor their interests over collective ones. The new peacemaker must constantly face the reality that these elites appear to be blind to the rigid orthodoxy of their own narrow conceptions of progress. From the perspective of the peace activist, there is a soul loss, as well as concealed depression, in the vision that the goal of existence is material progress and ever-accelerating consumption. The subtext of this aggressive materialist worldview is that our destiny is to become the servant of things—because as long as we serve things, they will keep us fed and entertained, and we can pretend that our stuff serves us. In this worldview, you have to be *really serious* about making money in order to be free enough to get all the things you want! Progress has become a hamster wheel of acquiring more stuff—at almost any cost, it seems. And let us not pretend that this view of reality is not an inherently violent one as it pollutes and degrades the environment, exploits labor, and conducts proxy wars for resources.

Peace activists now seek to throw this deadly and servile seriousness on its head and to affirm the centrality of conviviality, reciprocity, communion with nature, and collective nurturance. When these elements combine with values-oriented collaboration, creative expression, and the exploration of the higher capacities of consciousness, the peace movement will become unstoppable. What the emerging peacebuilder is dedicated to is nothing less than a system-wide *culture of peace*. Think of this entire cultural reframing around peace as evolutionary transformation rather than as imposed revolutionary thought forms or a forced change. The difference is that we become *evolutionary change agents* and *conscious cocreators* of our future rather than servants of illusory progress or angry protesters narrowly devoted to opposing the worst excesses of the status quo.

Anger is a tool, not a way of being

It is interesting that these two words, *cultivate* and *culture*, have the same root. They both refer to an active process of *tending*, as when one tills the soil. Peace understood in this sense is an interactive process that arises when we care for the world around us. When we pray for peace, we are asking for something that cannot in its essence be passively achieved. And when cultivating peace, we are anything but passive.

In cultivating peace, we are asking for a dynamic interaction with love, with gratitude, with forgiveness, and with cherishing.

In cultivating peace, we are asking that our true qualities engage with everyone and everything around us in ways that are fruitful.

In cultivating peace, we are asking for the force that dissolves any form of rejection, especially the annihilating forms of rejection that create emotional banishment and social isolation and that spiral into resentment or hatred.

Peace has the capacity to blow like a great wind of change that transforms the entire social order, but it begins with a breeze that must stir in the center of our own being. If that stirring is cultivated in the heart's core, it becomes a uniting force rather than a dividing one. But if the core is charged with anger, anger will permeate the work, whether it is called peace work or social justice work. We cannot effectively be grounded in corrosive anger: it burns us up, burns us out, and harms others if it is sustained.

But please attend to the following nuance: let's not make anger wrong, for it has its function as a surgical instrument in peace work. What leads to enmity is *attachment* to anger. Attachment to anger uses anger to incite anger in others in ways that breed hostility. This is the anger that begets anger and can lead to violence. True equanimity is lost when this kind of anger becomes the primary mode of communication.

There is a kind of moral fury that is cleansing, particularly when the one who delivers it is clearly coming from a place of love and compassion. Anger can be strategic in the toolkit of the peace ambassador. It is particularly effective when directed at injustice. It is good, in general, to follow the principle of directing anger at blatant social injustices rather than at people. Skillfully channeled anger can ignite the conscience of people and spur them to act on behalf of the oppressed. Arun Gandhi told a class of peace ambassadors during a Shift Network training that his grandfather Mahatma Gandhi likened anger to electricity: if used properly, it can turn on a light; if mishandled, it can do great damage.

Another related principle is separating the actor from the act: condemn torture but seek to rehabilitate the torturer so that he never tortures again and so that the system that colluded in these crimes is dismantled. How often we rail against the perpetrator but in our outrage fail to deal with the underlying structures of perpetration! Demagogues exploit anger to promote us/them scenarios and to call for revenge without addressing the underlying issues. Any form of vengeance, even when dressed up in the law, is corrosive and regressive. It is like throwing sulfuric acid into the face of peace.

Let's face it: the surrogates of deeply unskillful anger take many forms, including prejudice, exclusion, and resentment. Look closely and you will see the scars of anger on many parts of the social body resulting from the treatment of minorities and the most vulnerable. As peacemakers we are called to heal those scars, and that means we must learn how to transmute coagulated anger and suppressed rage. Rage is toxic, while moral passion is generative.

We must *choose* peace, because by its very nature it cannot impose itself on us. The kind of peace we are referring to here has psychological, spiritual, intellectual, and strategic activist components. Peace is an advanced state of being and an equally advanced state of knowing that we must engage if we are to activate it in every sphere of our lives. Go far enough into cultivating peace on all these levels, and you will see yourself developing a smile. It is a sign you are resolving polarities and synchronizing your inner being with your outer work. Peace activists who have done great inner work and who are also engaged in courageous peace work in the world share this smile with one another. They know that behind its gentle transmission are great power, strength, and a passion for justice. Peace can bring serenity in the midst of struggle and conflict because it can help us tap into hidden reservoirs of power. When we dedicate our lives to cultivating peace, we learn to experience *power with* instead of *power over.*

Choose peace as a compass for your inner life and for every relationship in the world, and you will get the biggest wake-up call of your life. You will be called to become a fully integrated human with as much emotional range, spiritual insight, and centered activism as you can muster to unite people rather than divide them. For as much as it reflects the heart's deepest response, a consciousness centered in peace is destined to manifest itself all the way from personal well-being through the entire social order and to forms of enlightened governance that will guide the entire planet.

A peace movement emerges, reflecting a shift in consciousness

As I noted earlier, we are witnessing a tidal shift in consciousness. Some see it as a great planetary awakening of awareness accompanied by an extended capacity for empathy and collaboration. The burgeoning networks of people who share these new values, along with the accelerating global communications environment, are creating an unprecedented planetary resonance. We are collectively beginning to shed the skin of humanity's dysfunctional consciousness.

Here are key transformations defining the new peace movement:

We are moving from being locked into outrage at war and violence, or being defined as a protest movement, to creating a culture of peace from the ground up and the inside out.

We are moving from the reactive condemnation of others, arising out of a presumed superior moral position, to engaging in dialogue, listening, and drawing on nonviolent communication strategies.

We are moving from labeling those who disagree with us as the enemy to recognizing the inherent flaw in creating enmity as a peace strategy. In this way our work attempts to dissolve polarizing behaviors.

We are moving from a consciousness that is problem centered to one that is solution centered. This has a radical impact on how we organize. We are informed by our vision, and our approach is not always defined by the tactics or stance of those we associate with the source of the problem.

We are moving from piecemeal, feel-good, quick-fix interventions to whole-system maps and systemic transformation.

We are moving from a reliance on ideological frameworks to integral approaches that are embodied manifestations of peace at the individual and collective levels.

We are moving from an activism that leads to burnout and relationship breakdowns to one in which working for the cause of peace requires self-care and time for quality relationships.

We are moving from the battleground of proving who is right and who is wrong to understanding worldview transformation and identifying who the wounded are and how they can find healing.

We are moving from an obsession with punishment to the search for truth, reconciliation, and restorative justice.

We are moving from demanding rights to assuming our responsibility to create environments that promote rights and social justice.

We are moving from merely critiquing the absence of humanity in others to honing our own capacity for compassionate action, deep empathy, and authentic forgiveness.

THE
Call

This, then, is the sounding note from inside the heart of peace itself. It says, "Choose me. *Cultivate* my ways."

Feel the pleasure of love, laughter, and service to others. Feel peace as the presence of conscious and compassionate awareness. Step boldly to incarnate your belief in the power of peace to transform indifference and hostility. Never allow meanness a foothold when instead there can be an ample generosity toward others.

Keep your conscience keenly attentive to the subtlest calls to live in attunement with your own evolving moral imagination. The world is full of moral dilemmas, so listen with confidence to the voice of your higher self, but always be willing to reconsider the validity of your position. Know that you have been asked to walk the path of essence, always drawing deeper from your own essential qualities and allowing them the freest expression—even when cold reason would suppress them. Work ceaselessly to connect the disconnected.

It is impossible to say whether you will be scorned or rejected or even if you will be cut down, but know that the winds of peace will carry your work to future generations and that you will be part of what turns humanity toward its true destiny.

Any action that begins in the core of your being is one that unites with the Source of All Being. Look for that igniting point midway between taking yourself too seriously and being too casual about your gifts; it is here that peace arises and asks you to dance with it. Whether your first gesture is to still the mind, pulse a drum, raise your voice, or cross the threshold of an old fear or enmity, celebrate your choice to leave passivity and disbelief behind.

Keep faith with your vision even if people scorn you for being an idealist. Make sure your vision is big enough for the time we live in and that your execution of the vision comes from a place of humility. Learn to celebrate your vision even in the midst of great suffering, for your vision is an answer to the suffering you see. Peace is the healer of wounds.

For as much as you cultivate peace in all of its dimensions, it will cultivate you *beyond all recognition*.

Reflection AND Practice

For some, conscious work around smiling and humor is a spiritual practice. Smiles help activate that inner biochemistry of flow. Like laughter, smiling is a signal that it is safe to connect. We have all experienced at some point how a smile can create a shift when things are tense, when someone feels hurt or blamed, or when there is doubt or confusion about one's intentions. Some traditions even practice an inner smile as a way of cultivating a quality of energy that reflects ease and nonjudgment.

Smiles make a connection that is essentially peaceful. See if you can practice more intentional smiling to connect with others, signal acceptance, or reflect any number of emotions that thaw separation, objectification, and otherness.

On the other hand, do not use smiling to create a false positive. People recognize superficiality and know when you are being inauthentic. What we are really talking about here is cultivating a disposition that has a natural tendency to reflect openness and to offer caring.

For those of you with big plans to help change the world, this exercise may seem pathetically inadequate as a first step. But the real game changers are those people whose humility allows them to open up the relational ground of being with anyone. Smiles can disarm our sense of self-importance and help us climb down from our favorite hobbyhorses. Smiles have a mysterious way of putting us on an equal footing.

The inner smile is cultivated on the breath. You allow it almost effortlessly to radiate at the cellular level. Maybe you will find it dissolving some encrusted feelings of hardness and judgment toward others. Or perhaps you will notice some other blockage that is your work to deal with before you can be a truly skillful peacemaker.

Notice when your anger is directed toward a person rather than the things they do. Never direct anger at someone's being; always learn to separate the two. This skill is an integral part of being a peace ambassador.

Watch when your anger becomes generalized rather than specific. Generalized anger is toxic. Anger arising from compassion and a passion for justice must be directed at specific conditions that need to be addressed but not at specific persons. Learn to accompany any voicing of anger on behalf of the oppressed with specific recommendations for change.

Make sure anger is not the root source of your passion and that it is not much more than a device employed with a solemn intention to do no harm to others.

Do some reflection on what indeed is the root and driving force of your passion for peace. Your work here is to cultivate the kind of inspiration and vision that will sustain you. If your passion is solely aroused by what you are against, you will burn out.

If you get a chance, gather some friends for a cosmic belly laugh together. Have you noticed that when we laugh really hard, tears roll down our cheeks? Tears and laughter symbolize wholeness. In the end, I cannot imagine a peacemaker who will not be in touch with both tears and laughter, for our work brings us to the doors of both suffering and celebration.

Finally, cultivate friends and allies, for without them you will burn out. Without the support and conviviality they provide, you might find yourself getting much too serious. Real passion can be sustained only through wholeness, and that involves relationships with others. Friends, when they go the distance together, learn from each other and provide each other with supportive feedback. They help us experience what some spiritual traditions refer to as the Friend, which is nothing less than the spirit of intimate support and guidance and the place where our heart knows peace.

Review the list of points outlined in the section above titled "A new peace movement emerges, reflecting a shift in consciousness." How are you a part of a newly framed peace movement? Where do you have unique work to do? Where can you see yourself collaborating with others to accelerate this shift in consciousness? As you contemplate the transformation of self and society, where do you really feel the energy and the excitement of participation? You can be assured of this: you have many kindred spirits in the new peace tribe waiting to work with you. Look for them. They are *social entrepreneurs, social artists, and social healers, and they are spiritual, cultural, and political activists* who are manifesting profound creativity from the heart of a new vision of peace on planet Earth.

Chapter 2

~

Peace and Freedom
from the Inside Out

While on his remarkable voyages and travels, Marco Polo thought he had found the mythical unicorn. As he noted in his diary, the problem was that, sadly, the mystery animal was not fabulous or enchanting, as he had expected, but ugly. What he had come across was a rhinoceros!

We identify everything in the world around us in the light of our experiences and cognitive categories and in accord with our worldview, the superstructure of meanings that we hold to. Our subjective perceptions and our interpretations of our experiences are inextricably tied together in this viewpoint of our world.

Look closely and you will see that almost everything around us has a label dictated by our language and culture. If we come across something that is anomalous or mysterious, or for which we do not already have a label, we will tend to do what Marco Polo did: project our creative meaning onto it. Once we recognize this phenomenon, we are better able to step back from our projections to gain a more accurate picture.

But as the historian of science Thomas Kuhn famously pointed out, new paradigms can have a tough time breaking through even among "objective" scientists. That is all the more reason to expect that we all, scientist or nonscientist, can be imprisoned by what we think we see and know. We can even become quite dogmatic about our version of reality. Human history is crowded with bloody conflagrations created by people's attachment to their version of things. We fight over who is most objective and denigrate others' subjective experience as though it were inferior to our own.

We can get locked into our constructions of reality and employ a form of reasoning that relies heavily on a simple logic that demands an either/or approach to organizing meaning. Pushed to its extreme in situations involving social conflict, this becomes the logic of challenges like "You're either for us or against us!" "Whose side are you on?" or "It is simply a matter of right versus wrong." War, terrorism, and bigotry are anchored in this kind of logic. Nuance, subtlety, and ambiguity are crushed under the jackboot of certainty.

In this discussion, we already have gone from a consideration of mental labeling and how it influences our perceptions and forms our worldview to the structural dynamics of labeling that can end up in fierce divisions, animosity, and hatred. And yet, even though part of the world is in a winter of divisiveness, where righteous fundamentalisms compete for ownership of the truth, a global thaw has begun. We still have rigid political hierarchies and fiercely intolerant and even violent fundamentalist religions in so many places, but young people everywhere seem hungry for change. And in places like Syria they are willing to die to create truly pluralistic and democratic societies.

The slowly emergent new normal of human relations does not negate *either/or*, but it is also able to integrate *both/and* as never before. We live at a time of deepening complexity in the form of information and knowledge explosion, culturally diverse societies, shifts in rigid gender roles and identities, crowd-sourcing, and planetary cross-pollination. In a world richly textured by new-meaning creation on such a scale as this, the question Who is right? seems a little quirky at best. The questions that seem more apropos to our time are, Who are the morally coherent, and how do they thrive in the midst of chaos and complexity?

I have spent more than two decades in dialogue with remarkable people who transcend the lethal polarity of "You're either with us or with them." They consider themselves to be average human beings, but if they are, I like to think of them as the emerging new average. They find our deeper human identity beyond labels. These are people such as Maureen Hetherington from Derry in Northern Ireland. Maureen is the wife of a Royal Ulster Constabulary officer who had his arm shot off by IRA fighters. Maureen was pregnant at the time. You could say she was destined to see things from the Protestant perspective. Her bitter experience might easily have exacerbated her perception of who was on the side of right and who was on the side of wrong. She could have claimed the privileges of the victim and proclaimed her right to the moral high ground. But instead she decided to tear down the walls of her conditioned reality. She dedicated herself to seeking understanding. Maureen lives now as a leading voice for reconciliation and peace. She has come through enormous complexity and suffering to be someone who doesn't take the side of narrow self-interest. The place where she does her work is aptly named the Junction.

I wonder, given the example of ordinary heroes such as Maureen, what is your compass in relation to transforming polarized worldviews in your own life situation? What is your involvement in helping to shift perceptions governed by outmoded beliefs and archaic cultural mores?

I ask this because, in case you have not noticed, your attention is relentlessly sought by those who want to control social agendas. Whether subtly or openly, you are always being asked to take sides. How you perceive the other will make all the difference.

Your inner life is also the territory to be won over by voracious corporate interests and their political surrogates. The media is their pulpit as they seek to influence mass perception and sway opinion. Sometimes I get the impression they would have us still look for unicorns when at least some of us have woken up to find a hungry rhinoceros at our door.

It all begins with the process of identification

The process of identification is complex, but if we are to cultivate peace, we will have to understand it better. It holds the keys to freedom. Our problem is that, in our daily life, we use unconscious filters determined by the culture, ideology, and inherited beliefs with which we instinctively identify. We also operate with psychological, cognitive, emotional, and even physical filtering systems that we are usually not particularly aware of. Many of us like the idea of being ambassadors of peace until we discover that doing peace work requires us to examine how these layers of conscious and unconscious identification are operating in our own mind-body system.

When we start to do this work, we learn quickly that peace is not an abstraction, not something separate from who are in the moment. We become more aware that our emotions are triggered in certain situations. We are turned off. We get defensive. We get judgmental. It seems the body gives us detailed feedback on where we have work to do. We can tell people we love peace, but whether that is an abstraction or a reality is shown by the way our bodies respond during a conflict. Does our breathing get shallow? Does our mind go into a berating internal monologue? Are we really listening to the other person? Are we pumping so much adrenaline that all we are doing is giving off a hostile vibration? When it comes to what we are really identifying with, modern science tells us that we had better look at our personal biochemistry for clues. Behind every label we apply to others are nested patterns of emotion to deal with and easily triggered neural pathways that we have to reset.

We tend to identify with certain people in a positive and appreciative way; we always feel good around them. They activate a biochemistry of good feelings. Some people automatically arouse feelings of warmth, attraction, admiration, and respect. The same is true of people for whom we have an equally diverse spectrum of negative feelings. Feelings of dislike, anger, and distrust leave their own signature biochemical trail in the body.

For those of us who wish to be peace ambassadors, this is generally where we have work to do: homing in on the biochemistry of empathy and compassion and dissolving the biochemistry of animosity and contempt. This is where our inner work will affect our outer work. We must free ourselves of our identifications, right inside the cauldron of our own emotions, if we are to be able to help free others. How else do we really expect that we will have the power of a great peacemaker to stand in the fire of boiling enmity or fierce judgmental condemnation without getting triggered ourselves? How else can we "be the change" we seek in the world if we have not yet mastered our own triggers that lead us away from peace?

The front line of peacemaking is not only about identifying and changing the mental frames and filters we have about others but also about dealing with our whole body-mind reactivity to others. It's not just about changing the concepts that filter our intellectual perceptions; inner peace work requires us to do a lot of heavy lifting with our emotions as well.

The inner dimensions of our social relationships

If we are living a conscious life, we do our best to embrace positive feelings, and where we experience negativity toward others, we try at least to do no harm as we attempt to discern the root cause of our feelings. If we cultivate awareness, every feeling provides us with information that we can use for our growth. We learn that we can acquire deep emotional intelligence and gain the capacity to process difficult feelings, such as instinctive animosity and resentment. We learn that to be effective peace ambassadors we need not only a change of mind to break down stereotypes but also a change of heart to truly engage people once we stop labeling them.

Through this work, both mental and emotional, we can gain very practical insight into how we judge whether something or someone comes across as positive or negative. Peace will not be possible without the capacity to gain insight in this way, for it is through the conscious awareness of our body's signaling that we begin to notice prejudice and other conditioned triggers. Gaining insight into how we both personally and collectively select positive and negative categories, and attribute them to others in a social encounter, helps move us toward a much deeper connectivity with diverse groups and individuals. We start to understand why we withdraw from some people or even build fortresses to keep them out. We gain insight about our internal and often unconscious maps of who and what is positive or negative from four primary arenas: moral maps or frameworks, belief systems, psychological perspectives on our experience, and psychological shadow projections.[1]

Moral maps begin with our basic notions of right and wrong. Our evolving human story traces our journey in relationship to what is permitted and what is not permitted, what is just and what is unjust, what is humane and what is inhumane. Humanity has been steadily evolving universal principles that move us beyond provincial cultural ideas of what is acceptable or unacceptable at any given point. These principles include both the timeless truth of the Golden Rule and the emerging social consensus expressed in law and in evolving notions around individual autonomy and collective responsibility.

For as long as anyone can remember, an old moral order has struggled with a newer one. The needle of our moral compass may be guided by the brilliant conscience of outstanding leaders and religious teachers, but reaching the tipping point of a new social consensus that reflects high moral ideals in everyday life is necessary for sustained evolutionary progress. The peace ambassador helps to nudge evolving moral codes into mainstream reality so that this tipping point is reached. The most useful and influential maps of our moral development evolve toward the full self-realization of individuals and their ability to reflect universal principles of inclusion, collective solidarity, enlightened governance, and empathy. Consider what could happen when enough individuals reach this stage of moral development on planet Earth!

Belief systems arise out of our experience both *in* and *beyond* the structures of family, community, nation, religion, social and cultural contexts, science, academia, and so on. All of these contexts condition our beliefs about the nature of reality. Beliefs provide a much more comprehensive set of frames than moral codes do, and they determine how people actually behave toward others more than what people are told is the morally correct behavior. A pivotal role is played by thought leaders, spiritual leaders, political leaders, scientific explorers, social reformers, and other iconic figures who are involved in maintaining or challenging current belief systems. But their influence is receding as more people reach and surpass the consciousness of leaders distracted by ego gratification.

We live in a time when more and more people are gaining access to information and ideas beyond their local social and cultural contexts. This is giving them an opportunity to frame nuances in individual belief systems as never before. While belief systems are profoundly influenced by local contexts, we cannot underestimate the power of an emerging global context to reshape those systems. Our world is being unalterably transformed by the reality that communication tools are in the hands of average people. We now have the power not only to inform but also to influence one another's beliefs as never before. The peacebuilder lives on the forward edge of working toward a time when a global consensus emerges around the idea that peace is our destiny. And the peace we speak of will be a new collective high-water mark of all those inner-development capacities of emotional intelligence, psychological insight, and compassion synchronized with political and social structures that optimize human rights, human responsibility, and true freedom.

Our psychological perspectives on our relationships are shaped by the intensity of our experiences. Living experience, although heavily influenced by moral codes and belief systems, makes its own immediate and instinctive determination about right and wrong. It asks: Does it feel good or bad? Does it feel good even if I am told it's wrong? Does it feel bad even if I am told it's right? We learn to validate our own experience and not to rely just on abstract reason, moral codes, or inherited

beliefs. Taking a psychological perspective on our experiential awareness points the way to emotional freedom. Genuine psychological insight allows us to feel the texture of positive and negative feelings as
they arise and to gain clarity about where they come from. We begin
to see how trying to sustain outmoded moral codes and beliefs in the
face of the contrary results of our own actual experience causes guilt
and grief. We experience freedom and inspiration when we integrate
new beliefs that have been validated by accumulated personal experience. Then we learn to taste freedom as a richly textured and sensorial
reality.

Think of all the work the women's movement has had to do all
over the world to communicate their lived experience of their oppression by men. That work was a prelude to breaking through intense
social conditioning as women sought freedom from oppressive gender
stereotypes. In this sense, the women's movement and the peace movement are one movement, for any form of subjugation, oppression, or
prejudice is a form of violence. It long ago became clear that to achieve
their goals, women had to change the psychology of male domination
as well as women's own psychology of subjection. This is a great example of the sophisticated inner work needed to make our world more
fair and just and thus more peaceful.

In recent decades, we've witnessed an explosion in the modalities
of psychological insight and related spiritual guidance, much of them
based on scientific research, that help us explore why we feel good
about certain things and bad about others. We have discovered that we
have the freedom to reshape moral codes and beliefs in relation to the
integrity of our experience. We now see how love, altruism, forgiveness, generosity, and compassion create positive feelings and how their
opposites create negative feelings. I have witnessed the most profound
healing occur between former enemies when they gained true insight
into the way their situation arose because they were blinded by rigid
beliefs and conditioned to deny the reality of their experience. We cannot affirm too loudly the contribution to peacemaking that psychology
offers us in validating our personal and subjective experience.

Peacebuilders learn to *walk their talk* by homing in on this degree of psychological penetration. They learn how to regularly check their moral codes and beliefs against their real experience and then determine how new and more adaptive moral codes and beliefs can be put into action. The emerging model for peace activists is one of wholeness and balance in which they do the inner work to actualize the integrity they seek in the world.

Recognizing shadow projections is a fourth area of inner work that is vital to understand for peace work. The shadow so dangerously projected onto others in name-calling, and hate speech is a reflection of our own unresolved and repressed issues. In the psychology of peace work, we see the relationship between freeing ourselves and freeing others from projections that are often so damaging. As we do so, our conscience becomes luminous and our humanity more expansive. Imagine a world where everyone has reached the capacity to freely embrace difference without judgment!

When we see more accurately where the energy for positive action comes from and how this energy gets blocked and even converted into negative projections when there is a lack of inner congruence, we are ready to be agents of creative change. Some people call this *conscious activism*. From this perspective, we give priority to inner work because we can see the damage that we and others can do by using the peace movement as an avenue to vent our own unresolved hostilities and frustrations. As peace activists, we can no longer hide from the real work that requires us not to project onto others what we have not resolved in ourselves. It is easy to get into a mind-set in which all the problems in the world are on the outside.

Allow me to share my own early inner experience of working with shadow projection. At one time, I had what I thought was almost limitless energy to berate the governments responsible for human rights abuses. I testified before Congress, met government leaders from the United States and dozens of other countries, chastised the abusers in the media, spoke at endless conferences, and attended such things as the World Conference on Human Rights. I felt safe in my convictions and confident of the moral high ground that kept me busily seeking the prosecution of human rights violators. But after a decade of high-profile work in that arena, I was slowly running out of moral outrage. I began to see that we will never fix on the outside what is broken on the inside. I began to feel that as brilliant as our efforts to end human rights violations were, they were not addressing the root causes. My colleagues and I were dealing with the legal dimensions of violations without addressing the deeper psychological dimensions. We were not sufficiently aware of the roles of our own moral maps, personal beliefs, and shadow projections, nor of these same inner dimensions in those we considered to be the perpetrators.

After I left Amnesty International, I began to explore this whole terrain of wounding and healing and how to discern the root psychological causes of so many conflicts. Along with Dr. Judith Thompson, who is now codirector of the Social Healing Project, I launched dialogues on compassion and social healing with those who had survived conflict and devastating violations. We went deep into the heart of human suffering and trauma, into the wounds transmitted through belief, and into the psychology of healing. We went into the inner world for answers.

What I discovered is when we commit to this inner work, we find that we exacerbate friction with "the other" to the extent that we are unaware either of our own shadow material or of how certain beliefs we perceive as positive may be viewed by others as negative. In other words, much as they become sensitive to external signals and behavioral cues, peacebuilders must also become *active witnesses of their inner process*. This is a great shift, and one that requires mature practice.

Scale up this concept, and you may be able to see the problem of projection even more clearly. We can see how nations draw strength by encouraging patriotic feelings, national pride, and loyalty. This is not unhealthy until it reaches the stage of nationalist fervor, when looking at the state's weaknesses and inadequacies becomes anathema. We know that trouble looms when a nation projects only its positive aspects and forbids scrutiny of its negative ones. Extremism gets blinded by the brilliant sunlight of its own assumed perfection and becomes incapable of seeing any of its blemishes or imperfections. The terrorist, the dictator, the fundamentalist, and the demagogue closet the shadow, strangle doubt, and suffocate shades of meaning.

Healthy democracies need to be nurtured

History is replete with examples of devastating wounds suffered by the social body when the voice of conscience is struck down because it dared to articulate the morally untenable aspects of a regime. We see also how societies heal when questioning and dissent become foundational to a nation's process of recovering truth. Democracies have furthered the cause of global peace because, when they are healthy, they allow for deep introspection and debate. The work of the peacemaker is to help us identify with this potential for critical self-awareness in democracy and then to practice, practice, practice getting free.

The essence of this practice is for the peacebuilder to build the continuum from healthy personal introspection to societal introspection. At the personal level, when we process our own shadow experiences, the object is not to wallow in guilt and shame but to gain more integrity and to become a healthier, happier, and more effective human being. As we shall explore in the chapter on energy mastery, effective introspection helps us see how to process energy so that we can deal with our own blockages and not find ourselves mysteriously triggered by others. When we can transform the energy that triggers us, we are well on the way to being able to deal with the triggered aggression and threats of others. In fact, we can and should model how to successfully transform unhealthy conflict in our families, workplaces, and local communities.

The same is true at the larger societal level. The health of a democracy is in direct proportion to the strength and vibrancy of its ability to acknowledge and then to transform the kinds of conflict that can polarize people and even degenerate into violence.

The evolving peace movement understands that it must nurture the evolution of healthy democracy on a global scale; if it doesn't, it knows it will be spending eternity opposing war. It knows that when any form of national debate creates name-calling, bitter rivalry, or hostility, peacebuilders must quickly become active in creating contexts for the productive exchange of views.

Today's evolutionary peace movement further knows that when dissidents and minorities are scapegoated, it must come strenuously to their defense. Any effort to collapse diverse societies into monocultural expression leads inevitably to violence. Peace work is about expanding the capacity of a society to embrace multifaceted identities. Democracy is the best tool we have to align individual and collective freedom, but it must be worked at and slowly evolved. It is an ideal we must stretch for. Peace and democracy are a common signpost that says, "Take this path if you want to grow and evolve. Struggle to align individual and collective rights."

Democracy is vulnerable precisely because it seeks to maximize openness, transparency, and freedom. Peace activists must be vigilant in protecting it from those who would exploit its freedoms to subvert the rights of individuals or groups. Tending to the health of democracies and evolving them in ways that optimize deep and skillful participation by the citizenry is peace work.

Today's peace activists are akin to physicians and healers working to improve the health of the social body. They identify the systems, policies, and practices, on the one hand, that support societal health and collective well-being and, on the other, identify those that break up social cohesion, increase divisiveness, and become the equivalent of disease in the social body. When a doctor diagnoses cancer in a patient, she is identifying a condition that is negative for the health of the body, but the doctor herself cannot be construed as being negative. Unfortunately, those working on the ills in the social body are often attacked as though they were trying to do it harm. But the promotion of healthy social practices does not mean ignoring our obligation to oppose those practices that are unhealthy.

Studying the epidemiology of violence as a social disease and coming up with recommendations to address it are concrete examples of tending to the inner health of a democratic society so that it can authentically reflect the reality of peace. There is an international campaign to get the governments of the world to do just that—to study the root causes of violence in their societies and to come up with poli-cies and programs to mitigate it. The campaign aims to promote the establishment of national ministries and departments of peace that will take on the work of ending violence in society not by incarcerating more people but by conducting research, providing education, support-ing restorative justice initiatives, and addressing the social conditions that lead to violence. Too many democracies have proudly proclaimed their ideals while failing to address the root causes of their appalling homicide rates, gun violence, rape and sexual molestation, battery of women, and multiple forms of social and economic neglect, which tear at their social fabric. The emerging peace activist does not have the luxury of complaining about what is wrong with systems where these kinds of social pathologies are prevalent unless he or she is committed to help solve the problems. That means the peace movement will have to gets its hands dirty with the many initiatives it will take to sustain a healthy and vibrant democracy.

The emerging peacemaker synchronizes inner and outer work

The peacebuilder must develop an impressive skillfulness in offer-ing solutions, avoiding the blame game, and playing a mediating role between perspectives that are locked inside self-limiting definitions. While we are called to ignite the vision and passion needed to manifest a world transformed by peace, we can neither be missionaries of a new self-righteous truth nor Pollyannas who passively affirm that every-thing is going to be just fine. We must also be able to dance between systems perspectives and psychological insight. The attainment of freedom can never be a purely individual matter, nor can it be simply a systemic solution: the perfection of systems is inextricably entangled in an evolving story of human process in which the individual can influ-ence the system, and vice versa.

So what we must look at now are models that reveal a dynamic and interactive set of conditions in which the part and the whole are recognized as interconnected. We will look at the relationship between the parts and the whole in the chapter on systems theory, but for the moment, it is critical to appreciate that the old model— where the part is just a disposable element in a larger design—no longer adequately reflects our current understanding of how reality works. The universe is not a simple hierarchy. The more accurate term is *holarchy*, a system consisting of parts that are whole in themselves and yet part of a greater whole. Think of Russian matryoshka dolls: each doll is complete but held inside a larger doll. Scientists and systems theorists describe the universe as a series of nested relationships, but much more interactive and less static than dolls. We are inextricably part of the whole and just beginning to discover how our thoughts and inner world extend beyond us and influence others.

It should be noted that in this work of modeling how the inner and outer are interconnected, neuroscientists are playing an increasingly influential role. Science tells us that experience creates wiring: our neural pathways are like highways that carry the conditioned traffic of the mind and its interface with the emotions. Neuroscientists say, *what fires together, wires together*. Our neural pathways default to using the same established wiring to interpret our experience and to re-create past impressions. This is highly significant when we think about our ability as peace activists to change the dominant story. If our neural pathways were like an inescapable hamster wheel, we would be locked in by old habits and beliefs. The repercussions for the social order would be devastating, and we would collectively congeal around the rehearsal of the known and the inertia of our conditioned blockages. We would never be able to synchronize our inner world with changing conditions in the outer world.

But we are, in fact, designed for movement, progress, evolution, and new stories, even as we must recapitulate the wisdom transmitted to us by our forebears. As we gain new information, different perspectives, and fresh insight, we fire and wire new neural pathways; this phenomenon is referred to as the *neuroplasticity* of the brain. We are wired to explore, initiate, and create.

From the personal to the planetary, we are finding that individuals, communities, nations, and their systems can undergo radical transformation and change what once seemed inescapable facts of destiny. But to do so requires dedication to constant renewal and the cultivation of fresh insight into what is working and not working. This is equally true for the summoning of courage, which is to be steadfastly cultivated. We need constant courage to address the shadow side of our progress and the wounds we transmit from generation to generation.

Freeing our own inner lives and freeing the societies we live in have never been so clearly interconnected. Science, spirituality, and activist engagement affirm that embodying and living a peace practice is what sets you free, which in turn allows you to help free those around you. But that is where the real zinger is: you have to *be* what you believe.

If we really align our inner and outer, we will *be* courage and not just admirers of it. We will be like A. T. Ariyaratne, sometimes referred to as the Gandhi of Sri Lanka, who earlier in his career was tipped off that he might be assassinated at a large peace rally he had convened. What was his response? He went to the home of the big boss behind the plot, and he stood outside, shouting, "I hear you want to kill me. Why don't you do it now? That way we can avoid others being hurt or creating a riot." Not only was Ariyaratne not shot dead on the spot, but the man inside the house became one of his followers.

My friends, are you ready to *be* the change?

THE
Call

You are called by freedom to be free. You are asked to free yourself so that others might also be free. Your work is to dismantle oppression from the inside out. It is never a case of *all* or *nothing*. As you work on yourself, you begin to be a little more effective in transforming the world around you. As conditions around you improve and systems become more enlightened, you are naturally in a better environment to flourish.

Think of freedom as a ceaseless conversation between an internal reality and an external reality.

Remember that all conversation goes both ways.

Do not be oppressively judgmental of your own or others' inadequacies. Making others the guilty party is a way of putting the brakes on effective activism. When you see what interrupts or aggressively assaults peace in your world, make a choice not to meet it in the form of equal but opposite aggression. Rather, meet it with insight about the cause of its condition, the way a doctor looks at disease or a scientist looks at a phenomenon.

You are learning that how you identify people and situations is the key to freeing yourself from the addiction of having to be right or wrong. By cultivating the witness in your own seat of consciousness, you are actively developing your own capacity to move from reacting to symptoms to exploring strategies that address deeper causes. In this way, you see that peace work is social healing work.

Teach yourself and others how to recognize symptoms as symptoms and then how to distinguish them from their underlying causes. Take care not to identify with the problem or use the problem as the center of your organizing. First, get distance from the problem by identifying solutions. Recognizing problems is not difficult, since they are numerous. But solutions cannot be merely recognized; they must be actively conceived and imagined. Allow peace to be the center of your active imagination. Cultivate an ability to generate rich and hitherto unimagined possibilities. Free your mind to get out of the box of its conditioning, and paint fresh images on its subtle screens, like an inspired artist or director.

Cultivating peace is cultivating freshness, originality, aliveness, and the energy that can exist only in more perfect solutions. The problem, seen in isolation from its solutions, is loaded with entropy. Don't go down with it.

Do not confuse imagination with fantasy. Think of fantasy as the hamster wheel of repetition in your awareness or as something in you that is looking for more exotic versions of the same illusory idea. It is the daydream that is unable to summon new possibilities. Fantasy is not able to muster commitment, and so it evaporates. Think of imagination as original territory teeming with new life. Appreciate that its soil must be tilled by your audacity and commitment. See it as the universe's vast reservoir of unconditioned possibilities and evolutionary options. You are called *to reach for* these options. You are needed to prove that as a species we are ready *to stretch far enough* to not only envision but also enjoy the fruits of peace.

Remember that some bonds and ties are deeply oppressive and that other bonds and ties allow us to experience the fullness of our humanity. As a peacemaker, you are called on to help liberate yourself and others from the former and to deepen those that make the latter possible. Finding our freedom requires work at the spiritual, psychological, emotional, physical, and systemic levels. You are ready for these levels of complexity because your vision, through this work, is becoming deeply coherent, and your practice increasingly connects the inner and the outer.

Reflection AND Practice

Create an inventory of things you identify as having positive or negative attributes. This is not going to be a comprehensive list, but choose examples from a variety of categories. For example, write down what you identify as positive or negative in close family relationships, professional settings, social contexts, major political issues, economic and ecological concerns, the execution of justice, cultural mores, and so on.

The object of the exercise is to learn how to step back far enough so that you get perspective on how you identify positive and negative. Until you become a witness of your own inner processes, you will never be free. Certain core elements should start to come into view. Once you have your list, place the items in the following categories:

1. emotional or psychological triggers relating to your childhood or other unresolved issues
2. qualities emphasized in your upbringing or education
3. perspective gained from bitter or sweet experiences
4. inherited beliefs
5. a mature and considered worldview

Some people, for example, were brought up in a family environment in which conflict was studiously avoided. The implicit or explicit message was that conflict is negative and one should do everything in one's power to avoid it. People brought up in this kind of atmosphere can have a heavily conditioned response to conflict. They may have to work hard to experience conflict as neutral or productive. Real growth and learning occurs for them when they transform their relationship to conflict without suppressing the challenges that it can bring.

Ultimately, positive and negative are just two contrasting channels of information and energy. What is important is that we learn to read them accurately. We cannot be at peace or be free if we are held captive by either volatile suppressed negativity or false positivity.

You will find as you work with this practice that it has a great deal to do with personal and collective peace. While we can all agree in principle with the sentiment "accentuate the positive, eliminate the negative," we don't want to do that in reality. Just as conflict exists, so positive and negative exist. Believe me, the peace ambassador must be able to stand in both affirmation and negation. *No* requires as much moral courage as *yes*. What we are trying to do is to become conscious of how they operate in our lives and in society so that we can free ourselves from emotional reactivity and conditioned responses that no longer serve us.

When we really understand why something is the way it is— as well as why it should be something else—we create a foundation for cultivating peace. We gain the knowledge and identify the attitude needed to address the root causes of all the things that end up wounding us. We also strengthen the foundation of all that heals and makes us whole.

Whatever form of spiritual practice, prayer, mantra, or meditation you follow, work with it to remove your addiction to being right. The spirit in its essence is free, and it can teach you much if you listen to it. It knows stillness and movement, silence and eloquence, and the deep rhythms of expansion and contraction. It knows how to hold both conviction and detachment. It knows how to transcend polarity. It knows cosmic connection in ways the relentlessly busy mind cannot know. Ultimately you are invited to free yourself to be you. And when you are free, you are peace.

Chapter 3

~

Expanding Your Comfort Zone

Expanding your comfort zone is essential if you are to be an effective peace ambassador. If you are not profoundly committed to being stretched and tested, peace work may not be for you—although peacebuilding is not about forcing yourself to expand beyond what you are capable of. Rather, it's about taking everything that you are to a higher level and, in that place, drawing from a deeply sourced integration of your inner and outer worlds. In addition, effective peace workers learn to be comfortable testing their boundaries and then consolidating a greater inclusion of others, so that they constantly transcend their limitations and embrace difference.

For example, visualize Andrei Sakharov, a Nobel Prize-winning nuclear physicist, standing up to the entire Communist hierarchy of the USSR and calling for freedom of thought. Despite constant threats to himself and his family, he stood his ground and called for the end of the pervasive repression of dissidents. Naturally, he experienced some fear of reprisal, but what is most remarkable is how deep the certainty of his convictions was. Sakharov's conscience was a luminous force in his life. It was his greatest comfort, and from this secure place of inner conviction, his light expanded into greatness even when the cost to himself and his family was great. Sakharov exemplifies the greatest comfort of all: that you are living from, and prepared to act from, the core of your values. Most other comforts are trivial in comparison.

We all have safety needs, and security is a central theme when it comes to war and peace. Healthy relationships and the respect of our peers underlie the biology of nurturance and safety. We need to feel secure to reach out to others. We need to be able to draw on reservoirs of strength to step into volatile situations where people are angry or threatening us. Yet when we step beyond our fears, we often find places of solidarity in resolving enmity.

In the course of our evolutionary story, we have met such security and safety needs in kinship groups, clans, tribes, and nations. The challenge has always been to extend to others the comfort and protection we give to our own—whether it be tribe, nation, or even global community. We have developed a more and more sophisticated sense of *in-group/out-group* every time we have expanded the circle to include those previously excluded and disenfranchised. Every step requires individuals to muster the courage to cross the line that separates them from others and even when rejected to take comfort from the moral passion that calls them to seek unity over division. The story of peacemaking is about *the relentless pursuit of an ever-widening circle of inclusion.*

It is truly a mighty task to end all forms of disrespect, demeaning behaviors, attitudes of superiority, and prejudice based on religious beliefs, race, ethnicity, class, gender, sexual orientation, age, profession, health status, or income. Peace ambassadors are community builders whose vision of an expanded community goes from the local all the way to the Earth community. This vision is based on the legal, philosophical, and spiritual understanding that there are no lesser beings on the face of the earth.

Implementing this vision invariably means we have to shed our attachment to false and superficial comfort if we are to serve the greater whole in this way. To do so requires a commitment to the wholesale clarification of values and to personal transformation. Peace demands that we as peacebuilders value people more than the material stuff that supposedly makes us comfortable and that we put dialogue before the shallow comfort of dogma.

But we cannot venture into that new territory without a profound sense that it holds truly nourishing and expansive possibilities. We need to experience how serving the greater whole will serve our personal renewal as well as the greater good. We need to know that our service will not simply burn us out or leave us feeling more hopeless and diminished because of the challenges. It may seem cold comfort until you experience it, but we are renewed by living and enacting our deepest values—by really testing them in practice and not by merely articulating them.

All the world's religions teach some version of the Golden Rule— do unto others as you would have them do unto you. It is held up as a universal value. Yet it is often only the exceptional peacemakers who show us this principle in action. We are called upon to treat the vulnerable as we would be treated. We are invited to be like the Hutu woman in Rwanda. When her fellow Hutus came to her door with bloody axes in their hands demanding the lives of the Tutsis she was harboring, she flew into such a rage that they were convinced she had become a witch who had the power to curse them if they proceeded. Just imagine how our world would be if we actualized the universally taught value of the Golden Rule—even as applied in this radical example. The Golden Rule is not just about treating our immediate neighbors as we would have them treat us, but about applying the principle as a central feature of our collective planetary experience.

Only authentic peace carries the design codes to allow us *to scale up our values* so that we can envision and organize around collaborative models of planetary governance, economic sustainability, cultural plurality, evolving consciousness, and spiritual development. Peace maps a journey for humanity from the inner core of individuals to the vast social and political landscape of Earth's billions of denizens. Peace ambassadors are called to represent the audacity of a vision that calls us to global unity and that demands we knuckle down to the great work of revising the structures, institutions, and cultural mores that have thrived on so many elaborate forms of exclusion and myopic self-interest.

What do we truly need in order to be the change?

Peace asks its ambassadors questions such as: What is enough? Where is your true comfort found? How can you share your gifts and qualities to renew yourself and others in ever-widening circles of wellness, sustainability, and collaboration? How can you *be the change*?

I love the fact that after the financial collapse in Iceland, visionary peacebuilders organized conversation cafés that involved more than twenty thousand people in discussion about *values*. People felt betrayed by aggressive get-rich-quick schemes, but they also acknowledged that they themselves had participated in these schemes in the fever to acquire more stuff. Conscious of the ruin that they had brought upon themselves, they scrutinized their leaders and saw that it was time to look for a new kind of leadership that displayed honesty, humility, and integrity. They saw that at the root of dysfunctional leadership was a kind of hyperserious meanness and self-importance. They voted into office as mayor of Reykjavik a brilliant comedian, who also turned out to be a brilliant politician. In the end, once they had explored their values more thoroughly, the people found that they were safer with leaders who could authentically be themselves and not always take themselves so seriously. It is promising when so many people can sit and talk with one another and then make breakthrough choices.

The Iceland experience in organizing such large-scale public dialogue reminds us that we all need forums where we feel safe to be who we really are. We need those gathering places for kindred spirits. We need unstressed places where we can truly open ourselves to others, where we can commune and experience peace, where we can laugh and be deeply playful with one another—places where we can express our opinions without fear. These are the places where we can have some of our safety, attachment, nurturance, and affiliation needs met. The challenge arises from the fact that the fulfillment of these needs fosters a strong sense of physical, emotional, and psychological well-being.

The biochemistry is deeply pleasurable. But if we get too cozy and comfortable, we stop growing.

Peace work presents a dynamic challenge to expand our truest, most ethical, most convivial, most compassionate comfort zone and to go to inner domains far transcending any obsession with scrambling to secure the privileges we feel in the coziness of the status quo.

Nevertheless, we should not lose sight of the importance of meeting real needs. Fulfilling genuine needs is not a trivial matter. When our needs are not fulfilled, we become frustrated and anxious. When they are threatened, we can become very protective or even hostile and dangerous. To live in a state of peace and to represent peace in the world requires a dynamic and thorough appraisal of what we truly need. Otherwise our society may die of inflated and, in some cases, obscene levels of artificial comfort, while other societies literally starve or struggle to achieve the most basic of human needs. This scenario breeds injustice, exploitation, and even war over resources.

What adds to the complexity of the story of our needs is the way the delivery of security is tied to how we make sense of a world shaped in contrasting cultural contexts and divergent political systems and economic structures. It seems that only when people are ready, and conditions are right, can they rid themselves of military rule, monarchy, dictatorship, intolerant religious dogmatism, or ideological rigidity. Cultures go though their own developmental cycles. In 2011, enough people in Tunisia, Egypt, and Yemen had reached the point of deciding they had had enough with rule by dictator. Societal development theory has taught us that we can learn to let go of the comfort of relying on authority figures and instead choose greater self-reliance and self-realization, but only when the timing is right.

In the chapter on systems thinking, we will look more closely at societal development and in particular at the Spiral Dynamics theory presented by master teacher Don Beck. Spiral Dynamics sheds light on the complex weave in our social development between the fulfillment of an ever-evolving interplay of physical, emotional, psychological, and spiritual needs with societal structures of governance and institutional development. The peace ambassador is what Beck would call a spiral wizard—someone who becomes fluent in meeting people in their own meaning system and in identifying the conditions that need to change so that they can optimize their highest values.

As always, when describing the emerging peace movement, we have to draw a map that coherently links the personal and the planetary. The central axis of our development, both personal and collective, is consciousness itself and its interaction with contrasting local conditions and the rapidly changing global context.

We are at the dawn of a world ready to experience interdependence and then move on to true human solidarity and unity. But to be fully comfortable with that notion, we must see to it that the individual is not diluted or submerged in the collective. We must discover ways in which the collective can scintillate with the synergy and brilliance of diverse individuals and the emerging models of national and global governance that will best serve them.

Are you comfortable with your responsibility for the world?

Not so long ago in our development we thought our little planet was the center of the universe. Everything circled around us. That seemed logical and was hugely comforting. God had made the universe and had created humans on planet Earth as the center of the entire cosmic story. By then we had largely left behind the idea that the sun itself was God or that the heavenly bodies were feuding archetypal deities. Brilliant scientific explorers paid dearly for challenging such beliefs, but through their powers of reason, we have come to see the reality of a universe comprising trillions of suns and likely millions of Earth-like planets.

Some still believe that there is a literal heaven and hell and that God rewards us for good behavior and punishes us for bad by sending us up or down to these concrete locations. But it is not our task to drag people from the comfort they derive from such beliefs or to force them to accept others, in the way violent missionaries did in the past or fundamentalists or "nation builders" do in the present. We begin by living our own beliefs so vividly, authentically, and passionately that we attract dialogue and interest. In case this sounds easy, let me assure you that it requires courage, tenacity, and deep truth telling.

What we believe becomes our comfort zone, and all kinds of power relations, structures, and social contexts become entangled with our need for such comfort. Challenging outmoded beliefs invariably challenges the structures and vested interests that support them. As a result, many people are still trying to revise old dogmas in ways that will rescue these beliefs from evolution's compost heap, primarily because the beliefs are attached to these structures and the comforts they bring. *Shocking levels of violence persist because of the simple fact that some ideas rob other ideas of their power.* Much violence has been done through the ages when people have been forced to abandon the old gods and pledge allegiance to the new, all the more so when those new gods take the form of a "godless" ideology.

But there is hope: only in the last century have we begun to see that broader public awareness and new social and political structures can gestate a constant evolution of ideas that synchronize with scientific discoveries and dramatically reshape psychological and spiritual perspectives. We are slowly edging toward a more tolerant and less violent world with an expanded and more adaptable comfort zone. Globalization and access to information and networking technologies have coupled with the emergence of democracy, and this convergence provides us with advanced tools for forging social dialogue and consensus. All across the planet so-called average people are demanding full rights and participation in their political future.

The question we must ask is, where is the center in this new story? For the landscape that once belonged to solitary leaders is now crowded with a great multiplicity of voices seeking to be heard. Indeed, one by one all the forms of exclusivist power, privilege, colonial domination, and religious supremacy are unraveling—though not without huge cost or the equally monumental heroism required to dismantle these false comfort zones. The materialism once defined as the center of human progress is inadequate to the new task, because material progress meets only part of our needs.

Again, material and industrial advances are necessary. A hierarchy of needs no doubt exists, and basic needs must be met before others can be realized. The Global Peace Index, a product of the Institute for Economics and Peace, affirms the idea that societies that can meet the housing, health, educational, and basic income needs of their populations are less violent.[1] This fact is worth underscoring as a great achievement of material progress and free-market economies, but even given the achievements of relative material plenty, humankind still faces urgent issues concerning the planet's collective health and well-being, cultural plurality, social justice, ecological sustainability, and fairness in the global economy.

In search of a new global story for humanity

What many of us believe to be the new global story and the new center of organizing for humanity was certainly sounded in the Universal Declaration of Human Rights, but it has evolved further in **The Earth Charter**:[2]

Preamble

We stand at a critical moment in Earth's history, a time when humanity must choose its future [emphasis mine]. As the world becomes increasingly interdependent and fragile, the future at once holds great peril and great promise. To move forward we must recognize that in the midst of a magnificent diversity of cultures and life forms we are one human family and one Earth community with a common destiny. We must join together to bring forth a sustainable global society founded on respect for nature, universal human rights, economic justice, and a culture of peace. . . .

Universal Responsibility

To realize these aspirations, we must decide to live with a sense of universal responsibility, identifying ourselves with the whole Earth community as well as our local communities.

We are at once citizens of different nations and of one world in which the local and global are linked. Everyone shares responsibility for the present and future well-being of the human family and the larger living world. The spirit of human solidarity and kinship with all life is strengthened when we live with reverence for the mystery of being, gratitude for the gift of life, and humility regarding the human place in nature.

How does this new vision fit your comfort zone? Can you embrace this in a way that fits your belief system? The key memes provided in the Earth Charter include the following:

- *Rights* and *responsibilities.* We need to observe both, and we must map how they support each other in ways that create synergy among structures, law enforcement, and engaged citizen participation.
- *Local* and *global community.* We cannot abandon the local in pursuit of the global; more than ever we see the violence and dislocation that come from loss of community vitality and health.
- *A common destiny.* Never has our interdependence and interconnectedness been clearer; our destiny is to discover the depths of our unity.
- *Shared responsibility.* Every individual is a part of a resonant whole. To be human is to be called to make choices and decisions that will affect others; we are called to a consciousness that understands how each part has responsibility for supporting the whole.
- *The need to learn humility in the context of all life.* We are embedded in larger systems that, in our arrogance, we have begun to disrupt at alarming rates; we must learn to accurately perceive our relationship to all other life forms and the reality of our Earth habitat's eco-design.

You may remember that the Universal Declaration of Human Rights was to be followed by a single enforceable treaty, but ideological differences split it into two covenants: the Covenant on Civil and Political Rights and the Covenant on Economic, Social, and Cultural Rights. Governments of the West tended to ratify the former, and governments of the global South often ratified the latter. Ideological differences have kept most governments from fulfilling the vision contained in both. In addition, the retention of veto power in the UN Security Council, and the fact that the United Nations charter still enshrines national sovereignty, make it difficult to envision that the full panoply of human rights will be protected at the global level. Peace activists who combine the vision represented in the body of UN human rights treaties with that of the Earth Charter—particularly humility and collective responsibility—find themselves explaining a worldview that is by no means universally supported.

Those of us who are gathering around this new story use memes like global oneness, global awakening, consciousness raising, deep ecology, experiencing the global heart, new Earth tribe, global transformation, whole-systems transition, global commons, social healing, restorative justice, and spiritual revolution. This kind of language drives some people crazy and invites hostility toward those who hold these ideas.

To understand why opposition to this new center is so strong, let's shift from the planetary to the personal to explore how individual peacemakers are engaged in moving toward this new story in apathetic or hostile environments. More than that, let's examine how peacebuilders can engage in real dialogue about how we can live in peace whatever our vision of the future is.

Finding balance while expanding your commitment to grow

This chapter is called *expanding* your comfort zone, not *moving beyond it*. You may have to leave your comfort zone at least temporarily if you are going to meet people where they are. But at the same time, you always need to work from a center of renewal in your life. You need to be renewed by what is essential.

Deep comfort, derived from truly living your values and enjoying friends and family and all the things that nourish your sense of well-being, is not peripheral in peace work. It is the core. It is essential to have a center from which you gather strength, a center from which you can be generous, receive affirmation, and experience gratitude. Peace is an expansive field of reciprocity. Russian mystic George Gurdjieff referred to this principle as "the law of reciprocal maintenance."[3] The more you express and embody the reality of human interdependence in your personal life, the more you remove blockages and experience what is called flow. Getting your life's energies into that replenishing *flow* of giving and receiving requires great commitment and subtle practice. This leading-edge practice is also essential for a peace movement that seeks to carry the medicine of peace and not just its message.

We began our discussion of peace with smiles and laughter precisely because there is a kind of seriousness that kills, a moral frenzy that asks us to abandon our health and to weaken our ties to others in order to serve the greater cause. In times of great conflict, we receive invitations to join the anger brigades, feed guilt, or ride the waves of righteous fury. We can end up doing violence to ourselves and those close to us when we play savior to the world. It is clear that peace cannot be achieved by feeding compulsive behaviors, even when those behaviors are in service to a good cause.

I remember vividly how the death of the human right activist Iqbal Massih, a child of only twelve, pushed me toward that state of neurotic frustration that can proceed burnout. A year earlier, Massih had received a human rights award for his work in telling the world about the plight of young children shackled to looms as slaves to the carpet industry in Pakistan. I thought I had learned how to balance my human rights activism with family life and spiritual pursuits. But in reality I was stoking more moral fury than was healthy when I came home from the office after learning that Iqbal had been murdered. I tried to force my three young sons to feel the intensity of this outrage by interrupting them when they were sharing their news about scoring goals in soccer. I even directed a kind of recrimination at them: "Don't you understand how important this is?" One can be strangely comfortable in this kind of imbalance because of the emotional payoff from pointing a finger at what is morally reprehensible. It is easier to rage at what is wrong with the world than to attempt to sustain one's passion while living in balance.

Balance can combine outrage at the death of a twelve-year-old activist with a commitment to seek justice if one is also cultivating qualities such as compassion, empathy, and well-being in one's own life. Thomas Merton put it beautifully in *Conjectures of a Guilty Bystander*: "Frenzy destroys our inner capacity for peace. It destroys the fruitfulness of our work because it kills the inner wisdom which makes work fruitful." While the work of maintaining one's inner balance sounds less than earth-shaking, the peacebuilder is nonetheless called to cultivate inner wisdom more than moral proselytizing. Peace work is not about winning the argument; it is about mastering one's need to be the winner. When we can really put ourselves in the shoes of the other, when we can reach new depths of empathy, then we can be effective ambassadors of peace.

Empathy has attracted the interest of neuroscientists, primatologists, and social theorists, and in recent years we have seen the publication of books like *The Age of Empathy* and *The Empathic Civilization*.[4] The word *empathy* entered the English language only in the nineteenth century. Before that, the word *sympathy* was used. Whereas *sympathy* connotes "feeling sorry for," *empathy* is more suggestive of joining with the other or projecting yourself into another's situation. *Empathy* has a more participatory quality. Jeremy Rifkin, the author of *The Empathic Civilization*, points out that empathy is essentially communicative and collaborative and not oriented to finger-pointing and competition. Empathy invites mutuality and conviviality rather than righteousness. You are asked to comfort others and to expand your comfort zone to embrace levels of pain or trauma that you may find demanding. Empathy tests your ability to be stretched.

A whole book could be written on the theme of comfort, mostly because the concept has been invaded by commercial marketing and overindulgent consumption and self-gratification. Think instead of comforting others, such as the bereaved, the sick, and the dying. Think of bringing comfort to the homeless, to victims of violence, and to the depressed or despairing. Think of how the oppressed are comforted when they learn that you seek justice for them. Think of easing the pain and suffering of others so that they can drink an elixir of connection, love, nurturance, and ease, or experience the removal of oppressive conditions and hardships.

We all need this kind of comforting. In order to deliver it to others, we are not asked to abandon legitimate comforts we currently enjoy, which are human, generative, and licit. Rather, *the call is to expand our capacity* to cultivate peace and well-being in contexts where we would previously not have been able keep our balance. If we can expand the conditions under which we can sustain our own well-being, we will be able to extend that sense of well-being to ever-widening circles. What is not helpful is channeling neurosis into activism and presenting it as morally superior to lifestyles that are more balanced and healthy.

What do I mean by *balanced and healthy*? So much has been written on how to nourish health, to meditate, and to live with greater awareness that it would be redundant to attempt to add to it here. The whole mind-body health and integral medicine movement has generated a wealth of information and a significant body of scientific research that anyone looking for programs, practices, or techniques can draw on. A mountain of material is available on contemplative practice, emotional intelligence, relational skillfulness, and positive psychological states. This body of knowledge and practice is enormously influential as a foundational aspect of creating a culture of peace. As we proceed in this book, I am going to take it as a given that you are familiar with the key aspects of mind-body health and the basics of meditation or mindfulness practice.

Assuming that foundation allows us to focus on the work of building those connections between our own healthy and stabilized center of being and the emerging center of our collective becoming. For no matter how sensibly we are taking care of ourselves, we are probably lost in some degree of narcissism if we are not helping to care for others.

As we have noted, what we seek is an expanding center of comfort that fosters greater inclusion and that celebrates a new appreciation of a whole Earth community. That, of course, is where the hard peace work is done, because one person's comfort zone and another's are not the same, and in some cases are so different that they appear as irreparably separate instead of parts of the whole. Ultimately, one of the biggest things we have to get comfortable with is the nature of conflict itself, because peace is not about the annihilation of conflict. Peace is about making sure conflict does not degenerate into wounding or violence.

Clarifying your values and being comfortable with conflict

Deeply held values constitute the heart of a comfort zone because through them we derive psychospiritual and emotional nourishment. Peace work models how to engage creatively and nonviolently with conflicts around values and with divisions that can arise around where we declare our boundaries.

We live at a time when we can avoid publicly representing our values. With billions of people on the planet, we can melt into the crowd in ways that were not possible when we lived in close-knit communities. Life is a lot more complex, and we are often left on our own to clarify our values in a fast-changing world. Nevertheless, if we are to be effective peacebuilders, we are required not only to clarify our values but also to embody them. The problem is that when we get clear about our values, they will inevitably differ from other people's.

Here is a way to navigate this issue: Every value has boundaries. For example, if I say a central value I hold is respect for life, where do I establish the boundary on that? How far can I go with that principle? I may say that I am pro-life when it comes to the abortion debate but be pro-execution when it comes to the death penalty. I could also represent the opposite and say I am pro-choice but opposed to the death penalty. The boundary in this instance may be reflected in a host of variables: I could be opposed to abortion except in the case of rape or incest, opposed to executions except in cases that involve crimes against humanity, opposed to violent military force except in cases to prevent genocide.

The value cluster around reverence for life might have a boundary that extends to an opposition to eating animals, or a nuanced boundary that excludes killing mammals but not other forms of animal life, or an absolute, all-inclusive boundary that excludes the use of all animal products. Or this principle might include species protection and a range of values that have to do with protecting biodiversity. From just this one example, you can see that not everyone reading this will share precisely the same value boundaries. So, lest people come to blows over their differences, peace work looks for ways to create dialogue at the boundaries of values conflict. We will be looking at dialogue and communication issues later in the book; for now, let's get a clearer view of our own values territory.

By now our mantra is clear: the peace paradigm that calls to us is one that connects the inner and the outer, the personal and the planetary. We can expect chaos in the world if we lack clarity about our own values. That's why I urge everyone to do a values inventory. A values inventory helps to clarify what you prioritize in your life and where there is a disconnect between what you say you value and how you behave. There are both free and fee-paying sites online to help you do a thorough values inventory. Values-clarification work helps you see where your words and actions are in harmony and where unconscious blockages exist. Peace ambassadors are people who have become very clear about what their values are, how they reflect those values, and where they take action to further them. Remember Carl Jung's advice: "Until you make the unconscious conscious, it will direct your life, and you will call it fate."

Inner tension is the first thing you may feel in your body when either the core of your value system or your boundary meets another person's core or boundary. Depending on the situation, you may feel that exchanging contrasting views comes easily, or you may face a scenario in which both parties start to pump more adrenaline and harden their positions. The body always provides cues with a biochemical brew that tingles the solar plexus, speeds up the heart rate, shortens the breath, and reddens the face. If listened to carefully, the body will tell you to become conscious and not to descend into the kind of primal reactivity that will only bludgeon the other.

All of us need to learn how to ride the tension when we are pulled out of our comfort zone by another person's aggressive demeanor. We can do this, for example, by employing conscious-breathing practices and heart-centering work. We will cover aspects of peaceful communication in later chapters; what we are addressing here is the more fundamental practice of overriding the fight-or-flight mechanism. Focusing on breathing gently into your own heart and recalling someone you love has been scientifically proven by the Institute of HeartMath to reboot your system when it is pulled into anxiety or a hyperalert state. This simple practice alone will help ensure that you have the presence of mind to engage in values conversations without triggering your own unconscious freight or summarily dismissing the other participants.

Our bodies are signal stations and transmitters. Even before we know it, they are signaling attraction or repulsion to others. They carry ancient fears and desires. In this sense, it is our own consciousness that decides how to respond to impulses. When we make the choice to override our automatic triggers and responses, that means we have developed the ability to use the power of intention that informs the body to witness that we are choosing a new pathway, exploring a new possibility.

Two main roles have emerged for the peace movement in the values arena: in one role, a neutral party *creates contexts and manages processes* that bring people together for a fruitful values exchange or conflict mediation; in the other role, one *engages in sharing, organizing, and educating the public* around a core culture of peace values. We will cover this latter aspect in the last chapter, when we look at the leadership functions of the peace ambassador.

Let's examine here the first of these two roles: creating contexts and managing processes for values exchange is necessary at every level of peace work, from family to workplace, community, nation, and globe. Peacebuilders in this role help people experience *a safe ground of being and an environment supportive enough* that they feel free to express their differences. Peacemakers in this scenario endeavor to expand people's comfort zone so that they can move into spaces where they were either too angry or too fearful to go before. This is where you learn that peace work is about creating containers strong enough to hold differences. Search for Common Ground, a brilliant conflict-resolution organization, makes clear in its public materials that in conflict resolution, it is important to get beyond the notion that conflict itself is the problem. The problem is *violent or emotionally abusive* conflict. Conflict that leaves people flattened or demeaned is conflict that has not been managed well. The peace ambassador's work begins with the notion that conflict is neither positive nor negative; rather, it simply exists as a reality. How we deal with conflict is what makes the difference.

When we engage conflict constructively rather than try to avoid it, we cross the threshold into an expanded comfort zone where peace becomes a more real possibility. Our essential tools are nonviolent communication, dialogue, mediation, and diplomacy. But there are also numerous more subtle ways of signaling safety and building trust. Whether we are working person to person or nation to nation, we must first provide confidence-building measures and demonstrate sincerity before we can start addressing the heart of our differences.

Then, when we can truly engage with each other, a mystery unfolds: we enter a safe ground of being where we can share our differences and come to *know* each other. We can experience the balm of deep comfort in being able to meet others whom we had placed outside the bounds of acceptability for one reason or another. So often we live with a fiction of who the other is. When we come to know them in a peacebuilding context, it is not that we have to agree with them but that we can *appreciate* them for who they are. This alone is what humanizes the world and brings peace.

To expand our comfort zone we must decide to live in harmony with our conscience, even if we risk looking foolish or being rejected by those who are close to us. In choosing this path, we may become a solitary voice for a new moral order, a new science, or a new story. When Archbishop Desmond Tutu discusses his role in leading his country to choose forgiveness and reconciliation over violent revenge, he doesn't emphasize the courage the decision took so much as its having been an expression of his faith and his core being. Again and again in the social healing dialogues that I have helped facilitate over the last fifteen years, I have heard people talk about their profound altruism. Invariably, they say it came from tapping into a conscience so alive that it was the essence of who they were. The greatest act of courage may be to listen to and then act on that inner call.

We can all think of heroic beings who were able to stand up to tyranny with the kind of relentless persistence, creativity, and courage that are exceptional rather than normal. However, most of us live in a space where we are not directly exposed to such harsh oppression; instead, we must juggle many mundane priorities. Our greatest challenge is to become comfortable with the idea that we can make a real difference whether it is in a family squabble, an office dispute, an argument with friends, a local controversy, or any of the myriad occasions of conflict that anyone experiences on a regular basis.

In the end, peacemakers must become comfortable living in the fire of conflict and with complex moral dilemmas. They must be able to handle the pressure of engendering creative solutions more than ideological pronouncements. We do not have the luxury of rigid posturing, nor can we compromise values that we believe hold the keys to a peaceful, sustainable, and just future.

Peacemaking is sometimes thought of as the art of compromise, but in his book *Peace by Peaceful Means*, Johan Galtung, one of the master peace practitioners on the planet, reminds us that compromise often leaves no one happy. He encourages peacemakers to look for creative solutions that represent a higher ground.

The path to that higher ground can take us through landscapes of boiling feelings and all kinds of hurt and judgment, but the serenity that the peacemaker can acquire in the face of such difficulty is born of an indestructible sense that peace will be our collective destiny. Even if it is a challenging teacher, peace is evolving our capacities to go beyond polarization to find an elusive but real planetary harmony.

It is a mystery that we often have to leave our comfort zone in order to find peace. From birth we are pushed out of the comfort of the womb only to discover through struggle and life experience the greater comfort of becoming an adult in our own right. Peace calls us to shed the comforts that are partial, temporary, destructive, and illusory—admittedly, a monumental task, especially when we understand that it requires whole-systems transformation and a baseline of higher consciousness that we have not yet collectively achieved. But that is where the Earth Charter makes it clear that we are all being asked to accept *our* responsibility to play our part. Nothing less. It's on each of our shoulders to help transform a world unable to manage its conflicts. It's time to get comfortable with the idea that an unprecedented period of extraordinary growth and values transformation lies ahead if the human enterprise is to succeed.

THE
Call

First we are called to center, to locate our own essence. This is the place where it is safe to be you. If you dwell in your essence, you will know you are a child of a friendly universe that seeks to offer you peace in the midst of a world in turmoil. You are invited to hold your center of connection to all beings even as your mind experiences confusion and your heart's allegiances are tested. The path to serving a higher consciousness is not necessarily easy.

Contemplate the idea that the center is everywhere, as in the saying "God is a circle whose center is everywhere, whose circumference can never be found." Visualize the center as a place of unconditional love, acceptance, and peace, regardless of what is happening around you. Maybe the center is a mythical place for you; nonetheless, try to move toward it. Let the center seed your imagination.

Know that every time you sit above people in judgment, you are setting a boulder in your path, blocking your experience of the essential qualities of compassionate connection.

This does not mean you are not called upon by morality to judge immoral behaviors but rather that you are called to do so in ways that attempt to address their root causes and to bring about healing rather than vengeance.

Humanity is evolving toward a sense of planetary inclusion where no person or culture is on the periphery. You are not asked to be a missionary from the enlightened to the unenlightened but to work toward a value system in which each of us can grow and share our gifts.

You will meet conflict, for it is everywhere. Through successfully managed conflict, tremendous growth can occur. Seek to know and to understand those who stand opposed to you and your values. This is when you practice empathy, when it is difficult to stand in the shoes of the other and not simply when it is easy to relate or feel their pain.

Distinguish false comfort from true comfort. One is static, while the other is always stretching for growth. One is narcissistic, while the other invites deep reciprocity. Reach for the comfort of an active and a receptive conscience, and know that if you do so, this courageous action will allow you to step beyond your limitations.

Seek to bring comfort to those who despise you by offering respect and reverence for their being, even as you are called on to decry what you see as the injustice of their actions. To bring comfort in this sense is to live by and practice the Golden Rule: Do unto others as you would have them do unto you.

Do not dismiss anger or worry or fear. If you are open and centered in love, these emotions will be an expression of passion and engagement rather than the fuel of passivity or violence. Neurosis comes from stifled anger or unhealed wounding and serves only to incapacitate true passionate engagement.

Allow yourself to believe that if you come from an ample and generous space, you are helping to open up something deeper than winning an argument or converting someone to your viewpoint. Instead, you are expanding the sense of self and other. You are building community from the inside out. You are offering to end the fixation with *me* and to serve the joy of *we*. You are embodying reciprocal flow and the reality of human interdependence.

When you can stand in the fire of opposing views and feel whole, you are truly a peacemaker. And when you draw the deepest comfort from the fact that you wrestled faithfully with every moral dilemma presented to you, you will know peace.

You have been given significant responsibility to manifest your part in the new story, and it may be that in a universe where consciousness appears to be entangled in the subatomic realms, your intentions and actions will reverberate more than you will ever know.

Reflection AND Practice

Set aside time to do a values inventory. Go from the general to the specific, and look at all sides of a given values issue. Ask, for example: What is my position on the sanctity of life? Is taking a human life ever justified? When is the use of military force acceptable? Are there any circumstances where abortion is acceptable or where the death penalty should be permitted? How do sanctity-of-life issues relate to killing animals? How do I express my relationship to the sanctity of life in my consumption patterns, lifestyle, political choices, and so on?

Here is a quick and partial values checklist: sanctity of life, service to others, political participation, resolving conflict, acknowledging mistakes, conscious consumption, cultivating well-being, use of military force, peaceful and nonviolent communication, freedom of expression, truth, compassion, social justice, relational healing, spiritual practice, and prosperity.

Try to answer the following three questions for each value in the list:

- What is my belief about this value?
- How do I embody this belief or value?
- What actions of mine reflect this belief or value?

What you want to get at in this exercise is the clear expression of your values, the ways that you express those values as choices and behaviors, and coherence in the boundary areas.

The boundaries are important because they are where values intersect. For example, I support freedom of expression but draw the line at hate speech. Why? Because hate speech may spark violence or create emotional fear and intimidation, which is wounding to those subjected to it. One of my related core values is supporting relational healing, so I am going to say that punishing hate-speech provocateurs does not address their attitudes and beliefs. I favor educational and dialogic interventions in such cases.

Go far enough and deep enough with your values inventory, and you will have a *conscious framework* to live by and be able to communicate *a coherent worldview* to others. This approach to values clarification is in line with the fact that free and thinking people the world over increasingly do not rely exclusively on religious teachings, political ideology, or indoctrination to inform their worldview. The emerging worldview is marked by peer-to-peer exchange rather than authoritarian transmission. Technology and the massive scale of social networking continue to level what was once top-down communication, and they are powerful vehicles for exploring emerging worldviews.

Social transformation is not possible when people who profess certain values do not think through or consciously live their values—in such cases, more rigid and hierarchical values tend to prevail. But there is also a problem with being too laissez-faire with your values. You are called on to be discerning and responsible for your choices. Your values were packaged by religious, national, racial, and cultural identities, and the package contains both outmoded and very relevant material that you have to sort through. Ultimately, this is a story between you and your conscience—but one with greater implications than you might imagine. Live your values vividly!

More often than not, we expand our comfort zone not so much by taking bold leaps to the very edge of our courage as by making persistent, incremental efforts to shed false comfort and to stretch for a higher, more inclusive truth. We need to ask ourselves: What incremental steps can I take right now? What signals can I give to show that I am genuine about dialogue with others? What actions can I take to confirm my commitment to not avoiding conflict? What am I doing to work through any number of moral dilemmas that surround me? Where can I embody empathy for those who are ostracized or rejected?

All these questions point in the same direction if this effort at stretching our comfort zone is to have integrity: a values inventory and worldview clarification require an action plan. Action provides feedback; values invariably get adjusted when the rubber hits the road. None of us has to be alone in all this. Numerous spiritual groups, community organizations, and social and eco-justice groups can help us take action. Any number of wonderful organizations specifically address values clarification and innovative action around community renewal and sustainability. Transition Towns, Bioneers, the Pachamama Alliance, the Association for Global New Thought's Season for Nonviolence campaign, and the Shift Network are just a few of those organizations that help bring values reflection and creative action together. I also recommend such online resources as *Yes!* magazine and *Kosmos Journal*. Wherever we go for information or inspiration, it's time for us to find our tribe and to expand our comfort zone!

Chapter 4

~

Ending the
Transmission of Wounds

Vengeance is not inevitable. I met Father Michael Lapsley in 2000 at a conference on compassion and social healing organized by my longtime colleague and mentor Judith Thompson. In 1990, Michael Lapsley was brutally maimed by a letter bomb, losing both his arms and the sight of one eye. The bomb had been inserted between religious magazines by agents of the Apartheid regime in South Africa. Father Lapsley's response was not to seek vengeance but to continue to work ceaselessly for the oppressed. He also went on to create the Institute for Healing of Memories. Located in Cape Town, South Africa, the institute "seeks to contribute to the healing of individuals, communities, and nations." Its work is "grounded in the belief that we are all in need of healing because of what we have done, what we have failed to do, or what has been done to us."[1]

Albie Sachs is another anti-Apartheid activist who similarly lost one of his arms and the sight of one eye, this time from a car bomb. Albie had been imprisoned and tortured and finally became the target of a bombing for his resistance to the system of abuses that constituted Apartheid. After the bombing, he received a note from his supporters with the words, "We will avenge you."

But he did not want to perpetuate the cycle. Instead, he wanted what he called "soft vengeance," a nonviolent response. "Soft vengeance," Albie says, "is the triumph of your life, your goals, and your ideals." Albie describes how, during the hearings of the Truth and Reconciliation Commission, he offered one of his former torturers his left hand for a handshake, since the right hand had been blown off. This man had just confessed his crime of torturing Albie. After the handshake, Albie told an interviewer in 2011, his former torturer was reported to have cried ceaselessly for two weeks. Albie said that was more satisfying than seeing him go to prison.

So many stories from South Africa reinforce for us the power of attempting to process the wounds of oppression rather than lashing out in vengeance and creating more wounds. The intergenerational transfer of wounds is the greatest threat to peace, just as it is the greatest cause of war. The challenge is that our wounding is not only transferred as emotional trauma; much of it goes into hiding inside the hearts of victims and in the collective awareness of a victimized population. Trauma can show up as anxiety, suspicion, fear, and powerlessness, but it can also be transmitted as hostility, rage, bullying, and abuse.

At the center of all such stories of societal wounding and its historical transmission are real victims and real perpetrators. From my ten years of working with Amnesty International, as well as living in places such as Beirut during the war and massacres in 1982, I have witnessed the extremes of torture and killing. My merely recounting them to you would be enough to give you nightmares. Very briefly, I'll share a few examples: I am haunted by the stories of Kurdish children in Saddam Hussein's Iraq whose eyes were gouged out to silence their parents; of a man who kept coming to my office begging me desperately, relentlessly, to find his three sons who had been disappeared; of a woman I knew who had been tortured with rats inserted into her vagina and whose son was later torched to death in the streets of Chile by official goons of the junta; of a friend in Turkey who was tortured for his writing with electric shocks precipitating epileptic seizures; and of the man who came to my office after spending fifteen years in a dungeon in the Atlas Mountains in North Africa, where a great many of the prisoners had died of cold or starvation.

That people can objectify others and subject them to insanely cruel treatment is beyond my comprehension, but I have spent years trying to understand just that. In some ways, the greater mystery is that a number of those who have been targets of extreme cruelty find ways to heal, to forgive, and even to reconcile with those responsible for their abuse. I have met those who have not only offered to shake the hand of their former torturers but also forgiven even those who murdered family members.

Such stories of recovery from devastating physical trauma, as well as deep injury to the psyche, offer compelling evidence of the indomitable nature of humanity. Here is where spirit can shine through; for where the shadow side of human nature is most intensely on display, spiritual luminosity can reveal an even greater power and strength, as with Father Lapsley, Albie Sachs, and so many others I have come to know.

In light of this observation, what is the role of the peacemaker with regard to interrupting the transmission of wounds? We earlier noted that since our survival instinct is genetically programmed, we may feel threatened by the beliefs and behaviors of others, which triggers a fight-or-flight response. When a perceived adversary does something that raises our internal threat levels, it may trigger a fight response on both sides that can be the precursor to violence or attempts at domination. As a result, we learn to read those fight/flight signals very carefully. Peacemakers, on the other hand, have worked hard to develop the capacity for exploring a transformative breakthrough rather than duking it out or running away, even if they themselves have been victimized. Standing your ground or defusing a threat requires courage, insight, and interpersonal skill. It also requires the wisdom to know the difference between overreaching and underachieving; accurately assessing when you are out of your depth is an essential part of the humility of a good peacemaker. All too often, the psychological profile of a perceived adversary may reveal levels of pathology or even psychosis, which need to be mitigated before an adversary harms others and before any other form of peace work is attempted. When dominating psychotics get political power, it is dangerous and naive to think they will be receptive to transformative dialogue.

All forms of violence need to be addressed by the peace movement: domestic violence and abuse; attacks motivated by hatred based on race, gender, or sexual orientation; structural violence and economic injustice; violent cultural practices against women; violence inherent in certain beliefs; ideologies that advocate violence, such as terrorism; human rights violations that involve the exploitation of vulnerable groups; the denial of indigenous rights; genocide, war crimes, and crimes against humanity as laid out in the Geneva Convention; civil wars and warfare in all of its forms, even if "legal"; and many more. All these forms of violence have one thing in common: the deep psychological and physical scars and trauma they leave behind in both victims and perpetrators. The aspect of this work that we want to focus on here is the need for a framework that shows us how to look at wounding and how we can interrupt its transmission to future generations.

The perpetrator is also a wounded person

With certain caveats, let us use the frame of "the victimizer as victim." For me, President Bashar al-Assad of Syria is a clear example of this. His father, Hafez al-Assad, was a ruthless dictator who tortured and imprisoned anyone who stood in his way. He slaughtered more than ten thousand people in one incident in the city of Homs. This legacy of perpetration was the son's education. When faced with largely non-violent democratic protests by his own people, Bashar followed in his father's footsteps and tortured and killed thousands of innocent men, women, and children. People who have met him suggest that on the surface Bashar is urbane and even quite mellow, but one thing is clear: the wound he carries comes out of hiding once he feels threatened. It is a wound so deep that it privileges self-protection over the murder and torture of thousands of people.

It is difficult to feel compassion for a man who has done so much harm to others, yet the tragic absence of morality in his father created a moral vacuum in Bashar's interior life. An emotionally crippled man like this feels weak, and his relationship to power is profoundly distorted. Unless we have some measure of insight into the human condition, we will remain content with superficial moral stereotypes. The path of peace requires us to go beyond simplistic versions of good guys and bad guys. Compassion needs deep insight into the nature of the human condition.

Deep wounding is everywhere we look. In a recent workshop I conducted with about forty participants, two-thirds indicated they had been either sexually molested or sexually abused. Many were able to express deep compassion for the perpetrators, even when they were fathers subjecting their daughters to heavy and repeated abuse. We came to see how the offenders were wounded themselves. In my work, I am increasingly finding that conscious people are more than ever breaking the cycles of transmission of wounding from the previous generation by learning how to heal it. Think about how much trauma, anger, and even rage will be prevented by ending these cycles of sexual violation. The road to peace clearly calls for healing not just the scars of battle but also the more intimate ones that we receive closer to home.

The peace movement needs to engage in a process of psychological penetration into all types of transgression by seeing each perpetration as a form of wounding of both self and other—rather than as the simple choice of an "evil" actor to be "bad." Healing begins with understanding that the perpetrator acts out because of a trauma inherited from the past. But this dimension of compassionate understanding should never be interpreted as condoning reprehensible actions or as moral confusion. Again and again, we are called on to separate actor from action.

Perpetrators are woven into the fabric of the human evolutionary process. Humanity evolves through every challenge because in the end our story as a species is about learning to be more skillful in settling our disputes and acquiring the capacity to be more forgiving and compassionate. We have, for example, evolved to a place where a political form like dictatorship is no longer acceptable to most people because their consciousness has evolved beyond it. We know collectively that the only political forms that will thrive are authentic reflections of the will of the people.

My friend Sequoyah Trueblood, a Choctaw, would say that the story of our evolving consciousness is a story of healing the unresolved wounds of our predecessors. He believes that this work can be accomplished only when we drop our need to promote judgmental attitudes about perpetrators. It is only by practicing a rigorous commitment to nonjudgment that we can contribute to collective healing. Much as we have shown a devastating capacity for violence and brutality, our elders constantly remind us that this world was designed for healing. As we heal, we create a new and a healthier social space to operate in, which offers us new opportunities for free and creative expression.

Of course, healing is not just about interpersonal relations; it is also about healing throughout the social order, as we see how and where our wounds lead to economic exploitation, environmental degradation, and gross political manipulation. Our wounds, it seems, go untreated when they hide out in the heart of our beliefs and worldview.

The wounds in inherited beliefs

As peacemakers our work is to understand what drives otherwise good people to do terrible things. There is no single answer, of course, and no magic strategy that can address the root of all violence. But again, we can begin our analysis by *reframing the conversation* and by seeing the perpetrators as profoundly wounded people. There is no doubt that belief itself carries and compounds horrific wounds to those who swallow the poison pill of racial superiority, class dominance, religious dogmatism, or predatory nationalism. Terrorists inflict carnage indiscriminately because the virulent nature of their indoctrination strips away the core of their ability to relate to the pain and suffering of others. Terrorism shows the extreme blindness to others that narrow beliefs, matched with a loss of social opportunity, can create. Those who learn to unwind such rigid belief structures come to realize that they have been infected with something like a psychological virus. In many cases it takes heroic effort and considerable support to dismantle such indoctrination.

The trouble is that wounds can be concealed within beliefs and projected onto others. In this regard, we see the casting of blame dressed up as pseudo-rational critiques of other people's ways or lifestyles, but underneath lurk fear, inadequacy, and guilt. No wonder so many therapists and social workers are the new face of the peace movement!

It takes courage to admit to yourself that your conscience is calling you to cast off an unhealthy belief. Depending on the issue, it can be very risky to do so. Releasing a belief can be painful and traumatic—which is why many try to play it safe by not bucking the prevailing order even when that order is oppressive. We are led in this healing work by those whose conscience burns bright and who surrender even their lives to help decondition societies from harmful beliefs formed in cycles of traumatic wounding.

Peace work strives to create environments where it is safe to explore conditioned beliefs, and it provides support for people undergoing significant worldview transformation. Unwinding prejudice or cultural indoctrination is essential peace work. Peace education develops curricula to guide us in dismantling divisive and reductionist beliefs, which if left unchecked result in gender exploitation, racism, bigotry, and other forms of discrimination. Those who develop these materials know that once you attempt to unravel any form of prejudice, you are going to open up a cauldron of repressed emotions. Beliefs have a root system that must be addressed.

Women have a great deal to teach us in this regard: all across the globe they have been casting off belief structures that confine them to subservient roles. They have spearheaded positive change by peacefully demanding equal status. Women are gaining insight into internalized oppression and finding their voice as they challenge dysfunctional beliefs about women in different social, economic, and cultural contexts and religious traditions. They represent the single greatest aspect of creating a planetary culture of peace. The wound that gender domination has created cannot be overstressed, and that is why it must remain a key priority in the peacebuilding agenda.

Like any other system reacting to threat, male-dominated hierarchies and institutions can react violently when women exercise their rights. Attempting to transform beliefs embedded in power structures can arouse the worst forms of perpetrator behavior. Let's face it, prejudice against women runs the full gamut from subtle to extreme physical abuse and unspeakable cruelty and humiliation. But instead of responding in kind, women have modeled healing and reconciliation strategies in changing the attitudes and behavior of men. They have helped men to see that machismo is not a reflection of reality, and in doing so, they have spoken their truth nonviolently. They have helped men to see that a vision of manhood that does not give men access to their own feminine side ends up wounding both women and men. In many cases, men who have gained insight into gender oppression have become women's allies in helping to dismantle it and to educate other men. Helping perpetrators to see both the wound they carry and the wound they inflict is the essence of peacebuilding.

Breaching the prison of abstractions

The new peace movement calls for healing wounds from the inside out and then cultivating a culture of peace on that basis. This new emphasis is a huge contribution to changing the entire game, since the underlying principles of new-paradigm peacemaking are *Healer, heal thyself* and *Peacemaker, be peace*. It is only from this place of integrity that the peacebuilder can assist communities or nations facing conflict. Philosophical abstractions about peace will no longer serve.

Some contemporary philosophers understand this and have clearly pointed out that living in disembodied abstractions is one of the great wounds of modernity. Alfred North Whitehead saw how "the merest abstractions" could be used to control people. French philosopher Jean Baudrillard went further and suggested that we have created hauntingly abstracted societies where the reality that our major symbols point to has been taken away.

Indeed, we live in meaning-orchestrated environments where it is harder and harder to separate the real from the fictitious. Baudrillard's work was one of the inspirations for the popular movie *The Matrix*. His ideas about modern society and those of many other cultural critics make clear that healing the wound created by living in abstractions is crucial to peace work. This perspective calls on us *to embody our thinking* in being and doing. As peace ambassadors, we must get out of the matrix of hallucinated projections and taste what is really there! It begins with restoring what living inside a mentally envisioned reality has cut off from us. Peace work is indeed deep inner work, but lest we get lost in ourselves, we must also remember the Dalai Lama's admonition: "It is not enough to be compassionate. One must act." *Healing comes from aligning being and doing.* When we act, we usually get quick feedback in ways that help to inform our next steps. If we stay in the mind, we can move from one conjecture to another without actually experiencing change.

Others have pointed out that this split between mind and body, head and heart, is reflected in our frightening capacity to objectify people and to objectify nature. In a world overflowing with things, real people and the wild forces of nature become data, statistics, and "consumption patterns." Nature is seen exclusively as a critical resource rather than a living system. This attitude inflicts a wound at multiple levels of psyche and system, and as a result, this *divorce from nature* is now coming back to bite us badly.

We have learned a great deal in the last fifty years about healing at the personal level. We well know that we need to integrate the mental, emotional, and physical aspects of our lives. Once upon a time, we went to a doctor and asked to be fixed, the way we ask a mechanic to fix a car. But today a doctor will examine our emotional outlook as well as our physical well-being. In a similar way, if societies are to heal, they need to examine their attitudes. As we noted earlier, the language of peacebuilding focuses on creating attitudinal shifts in a variety of areas. Although this approach sounds daunting and potentially overwhelming, it is also good news: peacebuilders can focus on aspects of the culture where their own passions, qualities, and skills can be applied. The ranks of peace workers includes parents, students, teachers, scientists, engineers, scholars, artists, journalists, musicians, social workers, therapists, health professionals, businesspeople, legal professionals, and the clergy and spiritual teachers, for all of us are capable of working on the front lines of attitudinal shift and societal transformation. Peace activists are no longer bellowing at the gates. They have breached the walls and are working inside systems, transforming them incrementally from the inside out with a focus on cultural attitudes.

Peace has the capacity to frame a worldview that supports healing the wounds incurred in our evolutionary story. Embedded in this vision is the notion that we are more than a collection of individuals forced to compete with one another for limited resources. "The survival of the fittest" can be true only if *fitness* is redefined to mean the most loving, caring, and compassionate. Since science has begun to affirm that these qualities are indeed the ones that match up with wellness and longevity, as well as evolutionary resiliency, we can get beyond the charge that those who think this way are crackpot idealists.

Facing the wound of cynicism

Let us now move on to examine another dimension of wounding. The wound that blocks peacebuilding ideas and ridicules them as naive is a deep and seemingly impenetrable cynicism. Cynicism is wounded idealism, banished hope, and subservience to a false compromise that demands we knuckle under to the so-called reality of the way things are. Cynicism is characterized by negative and self-limiting ideas that build walls around a garden of bitterness and frustrated desires. This is the kind of wound that hides out and masquerades as piety, authority, or pragmatism. Cynicism hides its vulnerability and is closely related to machismo in this regard. It cannot admit that it shields places where dreams and aspirations were laughed at, scorned, or bullied.

The cynicism that tells us to play it safe is pervasive. It feeds off fear and a hardened experience of the world and its dangers. But its self-proclaimed realism about danger is built of a heavy reliance on distrust. So it acts as a vicious self-restraining cycle and self-fulfilling prophecy. Visionaries know there is constant danger in the world but never permit that danger to rule them or to influence their behavior in ways that stifle creativity. Creativity is often threatening to the status quo precisely because it refuses to live inside false limitations, contractions of the spirit, or in social inhibitions that are part of the transmission of wounds. It is essential for peacemakers to rise to this call of creativity with bold new assertions about the nature of social reality and the possibilities that exist for humanity. Our task is to embody and enact what Gandhi referred to as his "experiments with truth." Some cynics will play at the *appearance* of experimenting with truth but will make sure not to disrupt the status quo or to offend their sponsors. We have to become skillful in breaking the illusions that cynicism so easily confects. We create a mere illusion of doing peace work—we express profound cynicism—when we simply rail against problems whose underlying structures we have no intention of addressing.

We do not need to dwell on the way politicians cynically exploit various trends to keep themselves in power. It is crudely obvious most of the time. The peace movement urgently needs to develop strategies to recruit emotionally intelligent and morally evolved people to run for political office. Alas, until then, politicians and petty demagogues will continue to insidiously exploit the public's raw wounds for cynical political ends. For example, despite much evidence that the death penalty does not deter homicide, politicians often support it because it has been a vote getter.

At the heart of much of our wounding is the cynical marketing of *otherness*. Reasonable disagreement is deliberately pushed to extremes so that certain parties can benefit from the polarization. Negative stereotypes flourish in this kind of environment. The cynic manipulates differences to exacerbate conflicts, while the peacemaker looks to create dialogue and collaboration where possible. One breeds an atmosphere of disrespect and distrust; the other takes the long road to nurturing respect and building trust. Cynics believe there should always be an *us* on top and a *them* on the bottom of the pile, so they conclude that they must manipulate perceptions at the bottom in order to stay on top. We know all too well that creating denigrating images, which can be delivered in subtle ways, eventually leads to violent social divisions. In the end, cynicism breeds a world of haves and have-nots to feed the vacuum created by the loss of faith in human evolution.

Hear me. Bottom-feeder corporations—much like unscrupulous politicians the world over—play with the envy of those who have key possessions, who are "beautiful," "successful", and admired. This brings to mind a Sufi expression: *You possess only that which survives total shipwreck.* When materialist fixations become an effective surrogate for the deeper reality of who we are as beings—with our need for love, bonding, and acceptance—we create a world-wound that threatens the very essence of the human enterprise. The beauty of the concept of a culture of peace is that it is understood that we have to re-create community based on human values and needs rather than on the consumption of stuff or the competition for dominance.

Peacemaking has increasingly directed work toward healing multiple forms of trauma. Dr. Jim Gordon, one of the original leaders in the mind-body-health movement, is now leading brilliant and innovative work with victims of trauma in war-torn places like Gaza.[2] I deeply admire professionals like this, who defy every form of cynicism to demonstrate that we can heal the bitterest of wounds.

Interrupting cycles of wounding

If victims fail to release their sense of victimization, they can end up reenacting their wound or projecting it onto others. Imagine a world without the intergenerational transfer of wounding and what that would mean for peace. Let me share how this is not just a pipe dream—that is, how it is truly possible to break the cycles of transmission, so that the next generation is not drawn into the anger, hurt, and resentment of the previous one.

I know three people who were shot in different episodes of political violence. What is particularly notable about them is that in each case the bullet is still lodged in the body, a constant reminder of their wounding. The perpetrators failed to kill them but left a violent calling card. If anyone had a right to seek revenge, it would be someone living with a bullet inside them! But in each case, the victim chose a path other than vengeance.

In the first case the victim was only fifteen years old. She was demonstrating against an occupying army when soldiers opened fire with live ammunition. The young girl received a shot in her thigh. Bleeding profusely, she got to a hospital, where they stanched the bleeding. When they asked for a relative, she gave her older sister's name because her sister no longer lived at home, and the girl desperately wanted to keep her parents out of the picture. They had prohibited her from joining political demonstrations. When she learned that the doctor would not be able to operate to remove the bullet because it was lodged so deep that removing it would do more damage to her leg than leaving it, the subterfuge began. The sister agreed to make up a story and had her injured sibling stay with her for a while. To this day, these parents don't know that their daughter was shot and that she carries a bullet in her thigh. How devastating it must have felt to conceal a wound like that and to be deprived of the care, sympathy, and attention such an assault normally requires. But this woman has never retaliated for her injury; she is now a prominent psychiatrist whose life's work is to help those who are scarred and wounded by the appalling oppression of living under the continuing military occupation.

In the second case, a friend was having coffee in a public café when a terrorist started shooting. My friend managed to get behind an overturned table but got hit in the back of his upper thigh. He lost a lot of blood before anyone was able to rescue him and take him to a hospital. This man is now involved in deep dialogue with those whom the terrorist sought to represent. He is a man of peace and reconciliation and not, as you might suspect, consumed with anger. He too interrupted the transmission of his wounding to others by transforming hate and violence into peacemaking.

The third story is that of a woman who was on her way to work as a civil servant in a conflict-torn area. She was hit by a sniper on a rooftop. Her life was in danger: the bullet just missed her heart, and she lost pints of blood on the way to the hospital. When she regained consciousness, she found herself in emergency intensive care. The doctors did not believe she would survive. The bullet was lodged near her aorta, and trying to remove it would have been far too risky. Weeks passed, and it became clear that she was going to survive. Imagine being told to get on with your life with a bullet lodged next to your heart! But that is what she did. Initially, she faced anger and depression, but eventually she made a heroic choice to overcome her intense sense of victimization and began to heal. She knew that to heal she would have to humanize her enemies. In fact, she went further than that; she became a force for reconciliation, dialogue, and understanding.

The velocity of each of those bullets is symbolic of the momentum created by the wounding of others. The bullets don't stop in the body; they keep traveling deep into the lives of their victims and on into the culture. When rape, for example, is used as a weapon of war, the act isn't only about unbridled lust but also about inflicting an intergenerational wound on the psyche of the target population. Violate girls, women, and even grandmothers in this way, and you transmit the wound into future generations, where it will breed bitterness, shame, and violent rage.

We cannot acknowledge enough the power of those who interrupt the cycles of wounding. Think of every arena of wounding and abuse that if not perpetuated would mean generations of children given a chance to carry peace to a whole new level. Can you see how this might be possible?

We have touched on multiple levels of wounding here: the wounds of violent trauma, the wounds that insidiously become part of our victim status and identity, the wounds transmitted though culture and belief, and the self-limiting wound of cynicism. At the root of them all is dehumanization, where ideology comes first, or dogma comes first, or materialist achievement comes first—anything but the sacred value of an individual and the power to transform even the deepest wounding. Revaluing this deep identity in all human beings is at the heart of the contemporary peace movement. That perspective alone permits us to unify in a spiritual movement, a movement within the evolution of consciousness itself rather than one with exclusively political objectives.

Moving to restorative justice

The growing interest in restorative justice as an approach to societal healing should come as no surprise. At its heart is the notion that damage to human relationships must be attended to skillfully so as to bring about apology, atonement, and healing. Simply taking vengeance against perpetrators, as we have noted, only perpetuates cycles of wounding; resorting to punishment as the only tool of justice is devoid of real social benefit. By contrast, restorative justice seeks to give much-needed support to victims and to involve communities in arranging for victim-perpetrator communication and relational repair. This wiser approach establishes the kind of accountability that will offer pathways to rehabilitation to the authors of crimes and misdemeanors.

A number of indigenous societies practice restorative justice. This practice arises from their deep sense that both the injury and responsibility for it are collectively experienced: they understand that individuals do not act in a vacuum; they are part of a continuum of relationships that are causally linked in any chain of events. Because the social order is experienced in this way, as a living web of interconnections, they believe that the community must participate in offering meaningful support to victims and take responsibility for helping perpetrators restore harmony. There is a stark contrast between this approach to justice—which requires active engagement and facilitation—and the punitive approach, which asks nothing of communities and divorces the offender from any accountability for restitution or sincere apology. Ultimately, the aim of punitive justice is to assess guilt and to have the punishment represent a commensurate injury to the author of the crime, whereas the aim of restorative justice is to restore health to all parties.

Ample evidence indicates that the punitive approach to justice is largely a failure: recidivism rates suggest that prison life reinforces criminal attitudes and behaviors. Former inmates have told me they experienced an atmosphere of fear, hostility, and danger that was traumatizing. If we want less crime, it is time we turned toward the opportunities presented by approaches that engage victim and offender in relational repair.

Initially, the restorative approach may bring up tension, fear, anger, and shame, and even stir conflict, but it does so to bring wounded feelings out of hiding. If we never had to face each other after transgression, we would never grow. Restorative justice offers both victims and offenders a chance to grow and in so doing helps to interrupt the transmission of unhealed wounds.

THE Call

You are called to confront the very foundations of fear and distrust. Fear is often the anxious neighbor of our wounds. Fear can be subtle and deadly at the same time. Name your fears. Don't let them go underground where they will keep old wounds open and raw. Expressing the fear of loss or the fear of rejection can help give voice to feelings that might otherwise surface in more unhealthy ways. The easiest way to inflame wounds is to generate fear.

Examine attitudes that subtly make others the root of your personal or our collective problems. Witness your own tacit collusion with beliefs that you know are not in integrity with who you are or who you are becoming. Remember that the wounds of the past often seek cover and hide out in respectable places, where they can slowly release their hurt and disaffection. Because a wound gets covered over does not mean it has healed.

Don't be tempted to fortify yourself so that you are never vulnerable. Be open to the attempts of others to reach you in new ways. Healing your wounds from the inside out does not mean you have to heal them on your own. Sometimes you have to wait until you have the strength to fully open. Look for allies. Look for those who are good at helping you to confront fears they see slipping out in some of your opinions or tendencies. Seek ways to do the same for others.

Remind yourself that it is rarely the linear truth of who said what or did what to whom that is most important. Rather, it is how those experiences formed emotional and psychological states that is important. Facts can be a prelude to unraveling perpetration, but we all have unique ways of holding and storing hurt. It is the pain itself that must be released, even as we seek restorative justice. And don't rush yourself or others into quick healing. As cultural anthropologist and educator Angeles Arrien reminds us, "Healing does not occur in the fast lane."

Develop sophisticated antennae that help you pick up the nature of others' wounding: combine empathy and intuition. Learn to decipher the tones and subtle signals of humiliation, shame, self-loathing, traumatic abuse, rage, numbness, and alienation. Don't psychologize others but rather offer them, when appropriate, something more valuable: your friendship. You are not the healer, but you might be a part of the healing. Think of healing as restoring and enhancing a sense of wholeness; it has nothing to do with fixing.

Look for ways to always value people over things, and find ways to celebrate that have nothing to do with consuming things. Connect with the community of life and let nature be a part of your healing. This is not a solitary journey, even when you walk alone. Most importantly, despite the fact that cynicism underpins so much of public life, learn to voice your faith effectively. Shed beliefs that no longer serve the truth of who you really are, but never shed your faith in humanity and the indomitable nature of the spirit to reveal the essence of our quest for peace.

The wound in the cynic carries an energy that wants to cut you down. Cynics will tell you not to be so "lofty." They will tell you to "get real," when in truth they are the voice of the illusion of our separateness. They will tell you to be "grounded," when they have abandoned the true grounding forces of nature. They will tell you that "it will always be this way," but their reasoning comes from fear and not from insight. They will call you names because they are losing their own identity. And they may do more terrible things. But your faith is not the old faith that wants to join an *us* to prove *them* wrong. Your faith comes instead from a great mountain formed by every soul who ever longed for peace or dreamed that peace would come. Your faith comes from climbing that mountain and the view it gives you of our wholeness and our oneness. Your faith comes from waves of healing love, acceptance, and forgiveness.

Each generation is given wounds to heal from the past. Look at the great healing work that was done to move the world forward after the suffering of World War II. It is truly remarkable how many wounds to the soul, psyche, mind, and body—wounds of betrayal, injustice, separation, and loss—successive generations have had to face. Your work is to open yourself to healing. Finding healing is always the beginning of a story and not the end of one, for healing spreads. It will go on spreading until all our painful evolutionary stumbling leads to our achievement of skillfulness in human relations.

You were born to begin this tidal shift toward planetary healing. Know that when you tap into healing personal and collective wounds in your family, neighborhood, community, or nation, you are changing the future by releasing the past. There is nothing quite so beautiful as the smile of one who has released deep wounding, whose presence lets you know that in the end you will always be loved and forgiven, even when it takes generations to heal. The day of nonjudgment is coming! Come on, smile. As much as you are called to witness the hurt, your assignment is also to confirm that there can be no peace without healing. Healing releases its radiance without trumpets and fanfare—you know, like a smile that lights up the heavens.

Visualize legacies of the harshest wounds and the most toxic resentments being interrupted by an unprecedented intergenerational collaboration that finally dispels the corrosive abstractions and hopeless cynicism that have locked us into an old and unforgiving story. See your place in that new story. See what hope and permission are flowing from you to those younger than you and what waves of celebratory connection are flowing back from them to you. See also the wisdom and grace that come to you from your elders and the energy of deep release, forgiveness, and honor that you can send back to them.

Know deeply that you stand in the midst of this intergenerational shift in consciousness as an ambassador of peace. Let your passion represent peace in every sphere of your life's work and activity, until the day comes when everywhere you turn, you meet the face of peace.

Reflection AND Practice

Your challenge is to identify the places where you contribute to exacerbating one of the many dimensions of wounding we have looked at. There is always a spectrum: from gender insensitivity to the oppression of women, from racial or religious intolerance to bigotry and hate, from excessive consumption to gross materialism. Evaluate where you are on the spectrum of these wounding beliefs, ideologies, dogmas, and behaviors. Then explore what you can do to improve your attitude or to change your behavior. Be specific.

You may find that bringing certain attitudes into your consciousness and witnessing them is enough to begin the needed change. Sometimes you will be surprised to find that even though you have evolved quite a bit, you still have inherited conditioning to deal with. But unless you cultivate a specific behavioral change or a new practice, scientific research as well as common sense tells us that you will probably slide back.

Remind yourself that effort begins by setting a clear intention and then by manifesting the intended change. Neuroscientists say we can open up a new neural pathway to reflect a new possibility in our lives, but it is only through repetition and enactment that a new pathway is securely established. Unresolved wounds are like a force of entropy, pulling us away from the very actions needed to resolve them. If you are to become an effective ambassador of peace, you need to be able to embody the momentum needed for inner and outer change.

Work in the subtle realms is also important here. Look at where you find yourself tensing up when someone or some situation challenges you to look at yourself. When do you find yourself getting defensive, brittle, righteous, self-justifying, or pompous? These behaviors are all indicators that you are close to shadow material and buried hurt. See if you can lure the shadow wound out of hiding by telling someone what you are working on. Don't cringe with embarrassment. Expose your vulnerability. Do as they bravely do in Alcoholics Anonymous: give voice to what it is you need to work on. Remember, hiding vulnerability is itself a wound—in fact, it can be a great wound that leads to violence and domination.

We will be covering capacities of the peacemaker, including forgiveness work, more fully later in the book. The core challenge for now is to go from abstractions to concrete or actualized behavior. Really evaluate what you are doing to enact your beliefs and changed behaviors. Where is your conscience asking for behavioral changes in your life, and where are you just one more highly informed, well-educated armchair philosopher? Apathy is a clearly identifiable wound, but its sister is knowing what others should do without doing anything yourself. Make a list of what you preach but don't practice. Now, remind yourself where you do walk your talk, and celebrate those actions.

You are being asked not just to pile on more commitments but to keep reorienting your life around core ethical principles. Here's one example from my own life: my core passions are peace, sustainability, spirituality, and community. I reorganized my life to live in Crestone, Colorado, a town of innovators, artists, spiritual organizations, and peacebuilders who attempt to prioritize for these same passions. Crestone is not Shangri-La; it has all of the stuff that comes up when human beings interact. But this community represents an attempt to incarnate certain core values rather than just talking or dreaming about them.

It hardly needs to be said that you are invited to release your own attachment to victimhood if that exists in any form in your life. You might find that unredeemed victimhood shows up in groups that share a sense of being violated or exploited. If you are a part of such a community, avoid group rants, for they only feed the illusion that you are doing something about a problem. This does not mean ignore any violation or oppression; it means do not allow it to govern your inner life in the forms of passivity or emotional violence directed at the alleged perpetrators.

Right action can bring relief and a sense of empowerment. Where are you taking right action? The spectrum of right action extends from public education, lobbying, dialogue, and peacefully confronting perpetration, to legal action, active protest, and nonviolent civil disobedience. Healing wounds means that we activate our power to change the old story.

Finally, where can you engage in dialogue with those who have wounded you or who are wounding your community? What can you personally do to humanize "the other"? Where have you personally ended the blame game? Where, in the words of Saint Francis, can you do more "to understand than to be understood"?

Chapter 5

~

Peaceful Communication:
Engaged Listening

Peaceful communication requires conditions supporting the development of a circuitry of reciprocal exchange, or what I also call the "circuitry of resonance." In conflict situations, there are many ways to provide such support. Much good practice along this line is being shared in the fields of peacemaking, deep dialogue, public conversation, and mediation. To begin our discussion of this aspect of peaceful communication, let's look at some basic ground rules of engagement when convening individuals or groups are locked in conflict.

First, the peacebuilder and other stakeholders must formally or informally set the rules of engagement and the parameters of those matters to be discussed. Rules can include the following: speakers cannot be interrupted; ideas, theories, and facts can be challenged; and no ad hominem attacks are allowed. Attention should be paid to creating environments of trust and respect and, where needed, confidentiality. Participants should be instructed to avoid caricaturing the other's position or demeaning their ideas. In both formal and informal contexts, protagonists should pay close attention to strident tones or provocative body language.

These rules of engagement should be communicated to the parties before they meet. In addition, "setting the field" at the outset with silent meditation, centered breathing, pleasantries, chitchat, and relational warmth will help activate the circuitry of resonance so necessary for peaceful communication. The peacebuilder should always encourage the parties in dialogue to express their desire for a positive outcome and a deeper understanding in order to set a positive tone and atmosphere. In addition, sharing food or even something as simple as having a beverage together helps stimulate a sense of intimacy and connection.

All such stage setting is geared to creating the biochemistry of safety and softer attention. The aim is to diminish adrenaline and cortisol in the blood and to replace them with DHEA, or dehydroepiandrosterone, a hormone that facilitates ease and relaxation. Too much cortisol and we may go into a narrow or hyper focus and miss softer cues, subtler signals, or nuances. The release of DHEA allows us to be composed enough to tune in to others more fully.

For more advanced groups, I recommend providing exercises for shifting the electromagnetic field of the heart into one characterized by "coherence." From decades of research, the Institute of HeartMath has perfected simple techniques of altering the field around the heart that creates physiological states; in these states, relaxed attention, connectivity, and limbic resonance are more possible. The term *heart coherence*, coined by the institute, signifies that the field around the heart is organized by love, empathy, and compassion; its recommended method to achieve coherence is highly effective and not difficult to practice.[1]

Setting the conditions for enabling peaceful communication is helpful, but learning the skills for navigating conflicted communication is essential. While we assume, for example, that we were all born with a capacity to listen, peacemakers must hone and fine-tune their listening skills.

Full-spectrum listening

Listening may appear to be a somewhat passive activity, but it is a vital aspect of mediation, conflict resolution, and trust building. In conflict situations, people may look as if they are listening to one another, but often they are giving superficial attention to the other person while feeling frustrated and unheard themselves. Authentic listening, on the other hand, is one of the essential factors that activate the circuitry of connection between two people who are attempting to communicate.

Here is a quick review of the kinds of listening I have come to recognize over years of trying to improve my own listening skills.

Transactional listening. This kind of listening, which involves a discrete focus, does not activate a deeper connection because it synchronizes with a small part of the brain to perform a simple task. For example, you engage in transactional listening after you ask the supermarket checkout clerk if she registered the discount on the organic bananas, and you listen for the answer. This form of listening is used for simple questions that have a linear right or wrong answer or that contain bits of information or facts.

Cognitive-process listening. This is the kind of listening you do in class when you are asked to track complex information, answer questions, or apply the material in a particular way. You listen, and then you perform. How you perform depends on the quality and accuracy of your listening. Here you use a lot more of your brain than at the checkout counter. Some limbic activity may take place if you have performance anxiety, but generally, emotional processing is minimal in this kind of mental activity.

Identifying the degree of emotional involvement is important because it allows us to see if the listening style is context appropriate. Is it a situation where you are looking to gather more facts or to decipher fact from fiction, or do you need to make contact with deeper feelings? Some people—more often men than women—can listen in a way that is oriented solely toward problem solving when resolving the conflict very often requires going beyond logic and involves unraveling a complex entanglement of head and heart. Sometimes listening for a mere fix is part of the problem. However, some situations require deep cognitive processing, and too much emotionality can cloud issues that need to be logically and rationally sorted out.

Emotional-outcome listening. Unlike transactional listening, which is mostly cognitive, emotional-outcome listening makes a connection between the midbrain and the limbic system to help you process feelings. Here again, the listener is focused, but with emotional anticipation. It's the kind of listening you do when the answer is important to you and likely to trigger the biochemistry of pleasure, distress, excitement, or any number of other positive or negative feelings. Emotional-outcome listening occurs when you are keyed up in a kind of vigilant listening as you wait for that cascade of delight or disappointment to flood your senses and reverberate with meaning. Children can be particularly explicit in expressing their anticipation of desired outcomes, while adults learn to camouflage their expectation, relief, or disappointment. This kind of listening is important to recognize in nurturing peaceful communication, because if someone is waiting for either a desired or a feared response, it blocks other possible outcomes of the encounter. Being able to read the other person's emotional-listening stance also provides the peacebuilder with a lot of information. Not only does this help you anticipate where the conversation is headed, but it also gives you the opportunity to address the emotional subtext of the interaction.

Postural listening. When people are in a debating mode or involved in a more complex discussion, they are engaged in what I call postural listening, which often involves both cognitive and emotional circuitry. Even when the subject of debate or discussion is intellectual or abstract, the ego can stir up all kinds of emotional manipulation or rivalry. You want to impress, or you fear looking dumb; you want to win, or you are emotionally invested in not losing a particular point. You could say you are simultaneously processing the other's ideas or arguments while also mentally rehearsing your own presentation. I call it "postural" because you are listening with a mental stance of comparing your views with someone else's. It is difficult to listen with full openness in this kind of listening because you end up filtering what is coming in through intellectual or worldview frameworks. This is the kind of listening people do in a contest of ideas, when they are attempting rigor and discernment about nuances or differences.

Postural listening can take a low or high form. In its high form, the listener is acutely and skillfully receptive to the other's ideas and is able to process them without ego attachment. Democracy asks that we hone our debating skills so that we reach this form of skillful listening that can honor others while genuinely and respectfully giving voice to our perspectives. In its low form, postural listening is exclusively concerned with getting its point across and winning arguments.

Inquiry listening. This form of listening is used in pursuing a deep question, exploring a theory, or engaging in philosophical or spiritual discourse. Whereas postural listening has an element of persuasion, here the emphasis is on discovery, where increasingly deeper questions are asked and the truth is allowed to be revealed without ego involvement in a particular outcome. Inquiry listening allows you to process potentially complex and demanding ideas without trying to force them into a previously established worldview. There is openness in this kind of listening, where fresh insights and new ideas further the quality of engagement and attention.

Heart-centered listening. Heart-centered listening is also referred to as compassionate listening. This kind of listening is deeply empathic. You seek to commune with the other person in a way that indicates that you are fully present to them. In giving your full attention and offering an emotional connection, you create a space where the other person can feel safe to tell their story and express their feelings as you listen in a spirit of nonjudgment. This form of listening helps calm anxiety and can even short-circuit amygdala triggers that activate the biochemistry of fear and threat.[2] We all have a basic need to be heard at this level of heartfelt depth. We also have a need to be accepted. Those who develop this form of listening capacity serve the cause of peace by opening up conditions where people can share the truth of their experience and feel accepted for who they are, sometimes for the first time in their lives. Heart-centered listening has healing power.

Integral listening. This form of listening represents mastery. A system has become integral when it has achieved the coherent synchronization of the inner and the outer. Integral listening synchronizes mind and body, head and heart. It arises from deep conscious awareness and remains open in the face of turbulent egos and emotionality. It is detached but not disengaged. It permits insightful silence and listens to its content. It is not reactive or particularly emotive, but in the presence of this form of listening, your whole being feels seen and heard.

As it must be clear by now, we listen with much more than our ears. We listen with our whole body. We listen with our attention, with our heart's receptivity, with our mental clarity and creativity. Intuition is also a kind of deep listening to the inner self. Science has paid more attention in recent years to gut sensing and gut feelings. What scientists call the enteric nervous system, the so-called brain in the gut, is sometimes referred to as the third brain. It is the place that gives us a raw sense of things well before reason has a chance to shut it down with linear arguments.[3]

Our intuitive capacities are an orchestration of the body's subtle antennae of perception, perceptions that may come from the primal sensing of our gut, the heart's sensitivity, or the mind's ability to read patterns and predict outcomes. In summary, we listen when we give our attention. We listen when we extend ourselves to reach for contact and connection. Listening is a dynamic signal that requires deep activation; it is anything but passive. In its absence the Tower of Babel rises, the media cacophony grows louder, and extremists shout to be heard. Without deep proactive listening, we live in a world of fragments where all that gets heard at the end of the day are rants and sound bites. Tragically, we often don't start listening deeply until it is too late.

Peacemakers learn to listen deeply to the unspoken call of the wounded; to conflict as it ferments beneath the surface of apparently quiet lives; to the pleas for justice from those whose voices are not heard; and even to the cries from nature itself, which speak loudly to those who have ears to hear. Our world is getting louder and louder, but unless we learn to listen, it will be left to the screamers.

Listening as a tactical and surgical tool

Every job requires a set of tools. Listening is a primary tool for the peacebuilder. Marshall Rosenberg, the founder of the nonviolent-communication movement, reminds us that nonviolent communication attempts to disarm aggression with a combination of skillful questioning and listening. If someone is confronting you in a threatening posture, he suggests that the most tactical question to be asked is, What do you need me to understand?

This approach makes a lot of sense since it can reroute the neural pathway of the aggressor, who now has to process a question. Not only does the question engage a different part of the brain, but it also reaches into a psychological fundamental: need fulfillment. We have a primary need to be heard and understood. Even if we are not being perfectly understood, our need can be largely met when we see that someone is trying to understand us. Why? When someone tries to understand us, they extend contact and communion at the level of being to being. And in the end, this what we are hungry for. We drop our aggressive or defensive attitude when we experience any form of intimacy with another being.

Asking someone about their needs or helping to clarify embedded or repressed needs is a signal that you care. However, we often do not activate these kinds of questions or listening stances because we tell ourselves that we do not have the capacity to help the other person. We shut down because we don't want to overextend ourselves or because we are acting from our own unmet needs. Do you ever get the sense that some conversations are really between *hungry ghosts*, who exchange a lot of words but do not feed their deeper needs? We do not have to feel that we must save the other person or meet all their needs. What we can do is help the other person voice those needs and be met by genuine empathy.

Believe me, opening the way for someone to give voice to the needs they have never felt invited to express can be like opening prison gates. I was in the presence of a former Nazi who felt he had lived in the dungeon of history until a daughter of Holocaust survivors, in his words, "threw a bridge across the abyss" by allowing him to share his experience in the Hitler Youth Movement and to genuinely seek reconciliation. When our basic need to be heard is shut out by the inability, indifference, or contempt of others, a part of our psyche is imprisoned. This imprisonment, which so many feel, is the invisible violence of a world too busy to be bothered or too concerned that if it attends to others' needs it will compromise its own. But if we do not free the prisoners in the basement of our collective psyche, they will eventually break down the doors and burst upon the scene to wreck the superficial peace we have created.

Since listening is a form of communing, it creates a circuitry of reciprocal benefit. In the mystery of our listening to others, we hear reverberations within ourselves. Have you ever listened to another's story only to discover more about who you yourself are? We are not separate beings divided by impenetrable walls. We are subtly porous, always seeping inside one another. Compassion is not a commodity susceptible to the laws of scarcity. It is a way of connecting with the oceanic tides of being. Compassion experiences the vast scale of being and not its lack or its limited distribution channels. In the act of deep listening, you attune to being itself and do not allow yourself to be distracted by surface turbulence. Make contact with that energy of the depths, and healing begins. When we open those channels of communion where compassion flows, we are nothing less than skillful surgeons of peace. We open up the place where truth can be spoken and heard. We create a space where the wound is lured out of hiding. We signal that it is safe to allow passion to be ignited without burning others with its heat. And we get to heal ourselves in the process.

Creating the conditions for listening

In peacebuilding work, you may sometimes feel that certain kinds of angry individuals are unapproachable or that you will simply be dismissed by people who hold opposing beliefs or who are more rigid or self-righteous in their views. Naturally, the first task is to wipe the slate clean where you are holding stereotypes about these parties and to urge others to do so as well. You cannot expect to get very far when you project onto others and treat them as a class rather than as unique individuals. However, it is true that creating the conditions for peaceful communication can be fraught with difficulty. There are techniques for setting up a more formal dialogue, which we will explore in the next chapter, but here we look at the issue at a more interpersonal level.

We must always begin the process with ourselves. As we have noted, peacebuilders are obligated to recognize their own triggers. When we are triggered, we do not listen to others, and we don't hear what they are saying because a biochemical brew has boiled over inside us. We are thrown into a cascading pattern of responses that are stimulated by the repetition of an emotional reaction that began somewhere in the past but is still operating as a loaded neural pathway in the present. As I point out in my book *Creative Stress*, we all have a default response to stress. We have a default response to certain political attitudes and behaviors and a default response to certain personalities. Becoming clear about those default responses, and how they can become reactive triggers that cut people off, is essential inner work if we are to be effective in cultivating peace.

So, the primary condition for listening to occur is making sure we are constantly clearing our inner space so that we are not boiling over inside or drowning out the other with our mental noise. How we achieve that may be through any number of breathing, focusing, and nonjudgment techniques, but it requires practice and more practice. We know, for example, that breathing slowly into the heart reduces adrenaline and that focusing attention on a person you love boosts pleasure and kindness hormones. The more we cultivate practices like this, the more we will remain calm in the midst of stormy conflict.

Another approach, which is more advanced, is to practice a kind of aikido to deal with the velocity and intensity of energy coming at you that has the potential to trigger you and cut off effective listening. I call this approach *engaging essence*. First, we set an intention to truly receive what the other is saying, not so that we agree but so that we understand them. *We attempt to come from essence and keep our attention focused on the essence of the other.* This can make for interesting dynamics and can take the interaction away from the routine spouting of opinions.

Let me give an example. While I was with Amnesty International, I was asked to speak at a large synagogue outside Washington, DC. The topic was the death penalty, which AI opposes universally as a matter of principle. After giving a passionate appeal for the end of the death penalty—during which I cited the execution of innocent people, botched executions, the cases of juvenile criminals being executed as adults, and the execution of mentally impaired people—I opened up the floor for questions. An elderly lady rose to her feet. She lifted her arm to reveal the indelible reminder of the holocaust of the Jews in Nazi Germany. Like millions of her peers, she had been branded with a number. She cleared her throat: a lot of emotion was moving to the surface from a wellspring of pain and suffering. "I don't think that young street kids or people with mental problems should get the death penalty," she said. The emotion began to rise. "But those Nazi criminals who took our people to the gas chambers, they deserve it. If any of them are still alive, I would personally be happy to execute them. In fact, I would personally strangle each one of them." As she spoke these words, she made a twisting gesture with her hands, as you would for snapping the head off a chicken. She remained standing, quivering, while she waited for my response.

There was silence in the room. I looked at her deeply, but I could not see hatred in her being. Finally, I said, "Oh no, you wouldn't! You are truly a beautiful soul. You wouldn't hurt a fly." The aikido worked: she blushed like a young woman being courted, muttering as she sat down, "Oh, stop that." My words and her response sent a wave of delight and relief through the audience. I had chosen to witness her essence and her humanity. After the talk, a member of the congregation came up, and his words touched me deeply. "I am for the death penalty," he said. "But what you did today was more important than that debate. You recognized and honored our dear friend and saw her beauty. . . . The very opposite of what the Nazis did to her. They wanted to make her less than the dirt. You recognized her nobility. Thank you."

We cannot force people to see the world through our filters, but the kind of listening we have been exploring invites us to notice that filters exist on both sides. We can listen perceptively to the part of us that wants to be seen and heard beyond those filters. A great listener will evoke our true voice and will beckon our essence to reveal itself. I have witnessed people who bore deep wounds begin to release their pain and pent-up enmity because, finally, they felt heard. In one circle I helped convene, torture survivors and victims of abuse shared stories for four days. The amplified listening of the group was so powerful that many years later I still hear how healing it was for the participants.

Listening is not monolithic, nor is it just a matter of opening your ears. Listening has dimensions, and it requires skillful mastery if you are to become a great peacemaker.

THE Call

You have more than one voice within you; learn to recognize those inner voices that speak from your essence. Your truth has a unique "dial tone"; learn to listen for it and cultivate it. This is the voice that carries the freshness and originality of your being, not the one that is so cleverly rehearsed.

Listening for the signature frequencies of one's own being is more than attending to mind chatter or skillful mental acrobatics. It is more than tuning in to the fluctuating tides of the heart's hopes and fears. It is more than paying attention to one's virtues or vices. This kind of listening to your being calls you to surrender to your own mysterious depth. It calls you to explore yourself as spaciousness, as showered with life-giving qualities and as full of surprise.

Practice a form of listening that dissolves blockages. To listen to your own heart, you have to develop a sensor that feels beyond your resistance. To listen to your mind, you have to decipher ego's little staccato voice and its chameleon simulations of truth and authenticity. To listen to your body, you need humility to avoid reducing it to an object. The body is part of a continuum of mind and spirit, and attuning to its voice expressed through sensations and pulses of energy will help you listen to its wisdom.

Listening is always a form of extension. Grow subtle tendrils of connection to other beings. Let intuition steer you into sensing opportunities the rational mind cannot see. Listen to the voice of nature, for it will cleanse your senses with its sounds and stillness. It will teach you how to cultivate peace by inviting you to be present in an interdependent community of being.

Listening invites. Make it a warm invitation. Let your listening be aroused and full bodied. Remember that your gut has an ancient antenna that tunes in to primal signals lost by the busy mind and the overwhelmed heart.

Tune in to the whole story as it speaks in words, in tones, in the body's constant commentary, in what is not said, in the subtext of social context and psychological states.

Listen as a creator, not as a file clerk. When you truly understand that the quality of your listening will affect the quality of what you hear, you will see that it is not passive at all. It has the capacity to peel away so much dead energy and to give life to fresh truth.

Don't listen like someone laying traps or getting confirmation for what you believe to be the case, but listen for the news that comes fresh from someone's being because you have opened a space for it to be heard for the first time.

You are an ambassador of peace, which means in the new story of human becoming, you understand why nature designed you with two ears and one mouth. When you really hear and help elicit the need that can't be expressed, you interrupt violence in the making. And more than that, you are playing your part in changing our collective story from the unskillful communication that demeans others and breeds enmity to the foundations of truly peaceful communication.

Reflection AND Practice

You undoubtedly know that some of the people you owe the most to often held back their own needs so as to benefit you or others. Their need to serve, express love, and nurture was greater than the need to increase their comfort. Great ambassadors of peace understand and live this principle in a way that makes them real game changers. Write a list of ten important needs you have in your life and then consider which are truly essential. Which give you that energy that becomes the rocket booster for others? But please don't make this a piety contest! Put sensuality or intellectual stimulation as high on your list as you need to. If you are listening deeply to yourself, you will reflect those needs that stimulate your juiciest creativity and liberate the life force within you.

The basic hierarchy of needs holds true in many ways, but the higher-meaning needs of evolving beings begin to reshape the map of "lower" needs. We must have food, housing, and security before we can expand and develop our need for respect, love, and self-realization. But in a conscious person the need to share meaningful relationships supersedes other needs in ways that demonstrate how people are more important than possessions and how joy can be experienced through serving a higher cause. Ego needs are shed in favor of altruism. Pursue that vital energy which tells you that the need to dance or sing or paint or design software or journey with a shaman is your path to service. Listening to the inner voice, which will invariably run counter to the mainstream, is the way to ignite passion and fuel a more meaningful existence. Peacemakers are not in it for themselves, even though they may take a lot of time to work on themselves. They are social empaths and altruists. It is this fundamental stance that orients them toward healing and reconciliation. How does your own evolving story reflect a dissolving of *me-first* preoccupations? How do the ripples of your life's work and choices touch on widening circles of connection?

Listening to others from this perspective takes away any lifeless sense of duty to hear what they have to say and replaces it with an energy equation that is about opening up reciprocity and flow. You tune in to that primal sense of our need to be heard and understood.

If you are up to doing a little research, review the types of listening outlined in the chapter and see if you can map how often you use or encounter a particular listening modality. Share your research project with others and engage your family, your workplace, or your church in a conversation about the quality of listening in those environments.

Chapter 6

~

Peaceful Communication:
Facts, Experience, and Truth

The game show host asks the tense contestant, "True or false?" A tidy sum of money hangs on giving the correct answer. We, the viewing audience, also feel nervous anticipation—will the contestant be right or wrong? From childhood we are conditioned to anticipate getting a reward when we have the right answer and not getting one when we don't. But our experience tells us that while some things are true and some false, and some things right and some wrong, life is not that simple. Our experience tells us that facts can be viewed not only from different social and cultural perspectives but also with wildly contrasting aims and intentions. Go to the heart of any conflict, and you will find the protagonists having a different experience of what is true and false. Once we, as peacemakers, understand this, we can help people in conflict focus on sharing their experiences rather than putting their energy into determining who is right and who is wrong. While we must have an unswerving commitment to obtaining the facts, getting to the truth of each other's experience is at the heart of making peace.

Contemporary science loves the topic of truth or falsity as it is revealed in our biology. Scientists have developed a huge body of research on how our bodies indicate whether we are speaking truth or telling lies. Our body language and eye movements give clues; our skin tensility, fluctuations in heart rate, and changes in blood pressure reveal our reaction to questioning; changes in blood biochemistry mark the presence of emotional tension or relaxation; spasms in the solar plexus and other less visible reactions of our musculature reflect nervousness. Scientists are even able to observe which parts of our brain we use to process a question in a straightforward way versus the more circuitous neural pathways we use to invent an answer.

It is good the body knows. Because our body is created to be a truth monitor, we often experience relief after speaking the truth, even when we may have been filled with terror to get to that point. Getting to the truth can stir up fear, but when we know viscerally that something is true, its presence offers its reliability to us in a way that uncertainty and obvious deceptions can't. Truth can arouse conflict by what it says to us or by what it implies, but once its veracity has been accepted in the body, it remains a secure reference point for our choices, decisions, and actions. In other words, we may react badly or well to receiving truth, but once we know it as true and real in our heart, we have a clear choice: we can either acknowledge or deny what we reliably know to be the truth. Conscience is a marvelous reminder of what we know to be true and of that which we deny at our peril.

Sometimes denial is compounded by repeated refusals to see or to admit the truth. When we switch off our inner guidance system in this way, we build up emotional freight. Once we begin to suppress that still small voice within, we start to forget that it is we ourselves who buried our inner truth under layer upon layer of numbness or unattended resentments. Fear also can become so toxic that it buries the truth in the caverns and recesses of our subconscious, where it restlessly moves about as a hidden director of our choices. Obviously, rejecting what is true can never bring us to what is real.

Peace can never be secured by denying what is true at any level, whether inner or outer. Admittedly, people can have different perceptions of what is true; they can argue over what really happened and who ultimately bears responsibility. But reason informs us that some facts are reliable and even incontrovertible. The truth can have many shades of meaning, but common sense dictates that we have advanced tools for collecting basic evidence to set the historical record straight about genocide, racism, slavery, trafficking, child labor, patterns of discrimination and injustice, and even domestic and workplace disputes. Demographic and statistical data are increasingly at the disposal of those promoting peace and justice. Check out the innovative work being done in this regard by the Global Peace Index, which uses multiple data points to assess the quality of human rights and freedoms with social- and economic-development indicators.

Human rights organizations gain their credibility by documenting with clear impartiality the facts of repression. Abusive regimes try to hide this level of factual truth. I accompanied Jennifer Harbury, the celebrated Harvard lawyer, to Guatemala in 1993 to search for the remains of her husband, the guerrilla leader Ephraim Bamaca. We had been tipped off that after he was tortured by a Guatemalan operative allegedly on the CIA payroll, he was taken to a remote encampment and murdered. With the audacity of activists and, in Jennifer's case, the need to know the truth of what happened to her husband, we arrived unannounced at the military outpost. The Guatemalan government could no longer hide the fact that several dozen people had been summarily executed and buried at this site. Later, when the bodies were exhumed, Bamaca was not among the dead. Some months later I was contacted by a Guatemalan who agreed to meet me and Carlos Salinas, a member of my staff, in a Los Angeles hotel room; he claimed that Bamaca had been taken in a helicopter and dropped in shark-infested waters. Sometimes the facts are never perfectly resolved, but the truth is clear. In this case, Ephraim Bamaca was tortured and "disappeared"—namely, murdered.

It is true that facts can be interpreted in different ways depending on one's worldview or political orientation, but suppressing the gathering of data used for the cause of peace, human rights, or justice is itself a violation of the rights and basic freedoms firmly enshrined in international law. Our task now is to consolidate the very best data gathering and statistical analysis so that we can accurately tell the story of a planet birthing a vigorous peace movement, while at the same time others on this same planet violently repress this burgeoning movement. In addition, more advanced data gathering points the way to peace paradigms that, undergirded by good science, can be the basis for a new generation of domestic and international policy making.

It is clear that we have always been called upon to rigorously defend the truth illuminated by certain facts. Fact: millions of Jews were exterminated by Hitler's Nazi regime. A small number of extreme right-wing anti-Semitic people deny or minimize this fact, but trained historians as well as informed people the world over apply common-sense rules of evidence to affirm the truth of what happened.

Even though we do not know the exact number of people exterminated by the Nazis, we do know it included dissidents and resisters, Gypsies and homosexuals, and that about six million of the total were Jews. If we were to claim that only a few million were Jews, that would be falsifying history and a malicious distortion of a truth that has profound sacred relevance to the whole human story. When we tamper with the facts to change the truth of what happened, we assault the very foundation of peace. That Stalin was responsible for twenty million deaths and Mao for over forty million must remain front and center in the human historical record as a truth of the despotic nature of Communist dictatorships.

Part of the work of peace ambassadors everywhere is to gather facts, amass facts, and disseminate facts that reveal a deep moral truth about a historical event. But one well-established fact should not be used to minimize the truth of another fact; facts must be used in proper context if they are to amount to the truth about a human situation.

For example, the suffering of the Jews in the Holocaust created momentum for the founding of the state of Israel: this has become another fact of history. But this fact remains a psychological and political barrier to acknowledging another fact: that Palestinians have rights and that these rights have been denied. Palestinians cannot reverse the past, but neither do Israelis have the right to deny Palestinians their future through a partial interpretation of the facts of the past. Palestinians ask that the truth be clearly stated: the creation of the state of Israel was, in part, achieved by denying Palestinians their basic human rights. As we noted in our exploration of wounding and healing, the open acknowledgment of the pain of others is essential to resolving conflict and to greater healing. So also is the restoration of the hidden facts that underlie the wounding.

Political strategy and manipulation are all about creating new "facts" on the ground through the use of power. Untold human rights violations and oppression have resulted from the efforts of powerful elites to create "irreversible facts" with regard to ethnic, racial, or religious control over land and resources. In its masterful decision, known as Mabo, in 1992 the High Court of Australia addressed the "facts" that were used to dispossess the Aboriginal people. The court accepted that the whole principle of *terra nullius*—an uninhabited land—was an egregious untruth. The court recognized that the Aboriginal people inhabited the land and that simply because they thought themselves a part of it and not the owners of it, they should not have been made legally invisible. Listen to the court's decision:[1]

> The acts and events by which that dispossession [of the Aboriginal lands] in legal theory was carried into practical effect constitute the darkest aspect of the history of this nation. The nation as a whole must remain diminished unless and until there is an acknowledgment of, and retreat from, those past injustices.

Now that is speaking the truth!

More and more we have the tools needed to set the record straight in such situations and to hold accountable those responsible for these manipulations and crimes. Great work is done by those government agencies, nongovernmental organizations, and media outlets with integrity that relentlessly document and pursue demographic data and firsthand accounts to secure the most accurate versions of facts that rogue governments, terrorist organizations, corrupt politicians, and exploitative corporations would rather see erased.

Clearly there are gray areas where getting to the truth is part of appreciating a complex equation. History is a dynamic process, and social conditions in one place will reverberate and create new facts on the ground elsewhere. For example, Palestinian refugees fleeing Israel and settling in Lebanon created tensions there that resulted in intercommunal conflict, massacres, and war. Causality is often not a simple linear matter. This is where major peace work gets done: in finding ways to appreciate the complexity of reverberating and entangled causes and effects. An Indian spiritual teacher once said to me, "James, don't be like so many Westerners who think that karma is simply a matter of direct cause and effect. The truth is always in dynamic relationship to multiple interpenetrating causes and effects." The analogy that came to mind was that actions are less like ping-pong and more like billiards.

Yet it is clear that we can also work to decipher root causes. Peace activists have to constantly make sure they are not chasing effects and missing the deeper patterns of causation. As we have pointed out, hidden wounds are often the real cause of behaviors that are rationalized in different ways.

Often it is deeply rooted wounding that causes people to create hostile new "facts," ignore past transgressions, or revert to a past where the facts were radically different. This is true at the personal level and at the level of groups and nations. Peace requires us to move on from those wounds by creating a new consensus, while societal healing requires both an honorable and truthful relation to the past and the will to forge an inclusive vision for the future. As noted in the Aboriginal example, the history of colonialism requires that the facts of the past be honorably addressed and that indigenous people's rights be faithfully acknowledged, but the fact of colonialism and its ravages can never be completely unwound. Instead, a truly postcolonial relationship can evolve between parties willing to engage authentically as equals in a relationship that formerly required one to be superior and the other inferior based on a denial of historical facts.

Creating contexts that foster healthy social emergence

The bridge to a higher ground that can deliver optimal advantage to both conflicted parties *requires the creation of new contexts for a healthy social emergence.* Healthy societies cannot emerge when yesterday's vanquished are waiting to be tomorrow's victors. Peacebuilders must have a vision of new contexts for social emergence based on reconciliation. Without a template, simply taking the side of the most injured party and defending its rights is not sufficient for building a bridge to new contexts. We must seek to protect the most vulnerable but work ceaselessly to hone a vision of peace that will address root causes of division and create inclusive solutions.

The facts of oppression scream out and motivate us to take urgent action against the oppressors and to defend the oppressed from further assault, but the truth of what will turn a situation around invariably calls for mapping a way forward that benefits both parties. This concept is hard for those whose passion for justice is so oriented toward punishment that they see solutions only in terms of prosecution of the old order but remain vague as to how to create the new order. Let me underscore that moral outrage is much less valuable if it is not accompanied by a greater and more vibrant *moral imagination.* By that I mean envisaging a truth that heals all those wounds that have the power to turn yesterday's victims into tomorrow's perpetrators.

The peace movement is recognizing that the work of the moral imagination is most effective when it is integrated with the work of the visionary *social architect.* The concept of the social architect has three aspects: social artist, social healer, and social entrepreneur.

Jean Houston coined the term *social artist* to invite us to think of the social order as a canvas on which we express our creativity. John Paul Lederach coined the term *social healer* to help us focus on all the work that must be done to release old wounds, enmities, and unforgiveness.[2] The concept of the *social entrepreneur* has been adopted in many places to mark the need for creative initiatives to turn the values associated with peace, sustainability, and justice into real social capital. Each of these roles—social architect, social healer, social entrepreneur—takes the facts about where we are stuck and turns them into a new truth about what we have the power to become.

As social architects, peace ambassadors are asked to represent an expanded capacity for truth telling. We are asked to speak truth from the standpoint of a more comprehensive awareness of social context and an aroused social imagination. This expansion in turn requires an ability not only to listen deeply to different perspectives but also to embrace a wholeness that eludes partisan persuasion. I emphasize this point because too much of what has passed for peace work has carried deep partisan antagonism. This antagonism may come from a place of frustration at prolonged injustice, or it may come from anguish over the suffering inflicted on others. But while these feelings may spur us on, they cannot bring peace, for in themselves they lack wholeness. Moral fury and rage can bolt the stable, charge off on its own, and become consumed by its own righteousness. Such anger invariably polarizes victim and perpetrator and the community around them and feeds off the reprehensible character of those responsible for offenses, without driving any energy toward higher solutions, reconciliation, or restorative justice. Peace work is about the balm of solutions conceived out of a persistent faith that we are collectively able to move beyond the dynamic of good guys versus bad guys. Our truth is a healing truth that embraces the many-sided truth about a situation of conflict.

Please do not tell me, "That is all very nice, but get out of the way for those who really have the guts and passion to do what is necessary to make change." I can assure you that I have seen no fire greater than the one into which people step when they are willing to drop their armature of rightness and to truly allow the pain and truth of the other to burn its way to their conscience and melt the hardness of their heart. This attitude is far from the new age emphasis on quick, easy, and sophomoric affirmations and the power of the positive, which has at times given genuine social healing a bad rap. The healing that I know and that I have witnessed with torture survivors, victims of prejudice and oppression, and even survivors of genocide is one in which the fire of intense suffering is surrendered and released in the presence of a larger space of shared humanity. To heal means to make whole by rejoining those parts that have been denied, separated, or ripped apart. Rearranging the wounded parts or affirming a false and premature vision of healing will not bring genuine healing or reflect the truth of wholeness.

Only that which is greater than the sum of its parts will heal. Only that ground of being which is more spacious, loving, and forgiving than the original ground we stood upon will open up the flow of healing. Truth and healing are thus inextricably intertwined because neither are static: to be completely healed is never an isolated occurrence; our healing involves other people's healing, which in turn requires that they share the truth of their own lived experience. Nor can we ever assume we know all the truth, for truth is what entices us to grow and evolve and not to sit in some static place of comfort reserved for the "know-it-all."

Truth process and peacebuilding

Something very important happened in Argentina in 1983 that significantly affected the role of truth telling in nurturing peace. It was the advent of what we call *social truth process*. As the human story has moved away from barbaric acts of vengeance and the crude triumphalism of the victor's right to exploit the vanquished, civilization has been increasingly defined by the evolution of law. After the Second World War, the Nuremberg Trials were one attempt to prosecute those responsible for crimes against humanity and to avoid wreaking vengeance on a whole society according to some less evolved notion of law, as was done to Germany after World War I. Since 1948, international law has greatly expanded in the arenas of human rights, refugee protection, and the prosecution of genocide and other crimes against humanity. War crimes tribunals have been established in some instances, and an International Criminal Court was established in 2002 by the United Nations.

But the National Commission on Disappeared Persons established in Argentina in 1983 was different. Its work was to investigate and report on the disappearance of more than nine thousand Argentineans during the military junta's exercise of power from 1976 to 1983. The full findings of the commission are documented in a fifty-thousand-page report containing testimony and documents retrieved from the military and security apparatus. The summary of the commission's work was published in a book titled *Nunca Mas*, which became an instant national best seller. Additionally, a synopsis of the commission's work, including extracts of the witnesses' testimony, was shown on TV, riveting the country's attention. The whole process was of major historical significance: average citizens throughout Argentina were given a window into the truth of what had happened in their country. Families devastated by loss began to learn what had happened to their relatives. The facts were established, but something deeper occurred: an entire nation was exposed to a new truth that will serve to strengthen civil society and protect democracy in Argentina for generations to come.

Since the first Commission on Disappearances in Uganda in the 1970s—a prelude to the more advanced effort in Argentina—there have been thirty-two such commissions in twenty-eight countries. A number of these commissions moved further than documenting and establishing the facts of the past; they intentionally set out to link truth telling and reconciliation. Argentina's National Commission on Disappeared Persons was an early breakthrough, but the most famous among these initiatives toward reconciliation along with fact gathering was the South African Truth and Reconciliation Commission, first convened in 1995.

The TRC linked truth telling and amnesty for certain crimes committed in the context of Apartheid. It deliberately included crimes committed by both sides so as to avoid victor's justice. More than eight hundred perpetrators were given amnesty as a result.

The TRC committees were broadcast live, and people all over the country heard graphic testimony of torture and killing. Among these voices were those of perpetrators describing their involvement in the oppression and those of victims expressing reconciliation and forgiveness. Those unfamiliar with the challenges faced by the TRC might want to watch a movie like *Red Dust*, which attempts to explore the complex elements of complicity and emotional trauma and their impact on excavating the truth.

The TRC signaled a change to a world that had expected violence and retaliation by the black majority after years of vicious repression by the white minority. The change was that healing and reconciliation could be attempted with the help of not just factual truth but also emotional truth. The change also included the examination of crimes committed by the victorious party, namely the ANC. Throw your mind back to the Nuremberg Trials and then forward again to the TRC; comparing these two models will give you a sense of how we can evolve beyond a limited legal justice oriented toward punishment by those who defeated a clearly monstrous regime but who were in no way open to exploring their own crimes against humanity, let alone to offering the possibility of amnesty to those who had committed crimes on the other side.

Archbishop Desmond Tutu was a cochair of the TRC. He and I were at a conference named the "Quest for Global Healing" in Bali not long after terrorist bombings tragically struck that beautiful island. Archbishop Tutu talked about wounds and how they can fester below the surface. He suggested that in such cases the wounds must be reopened for healing to occur. For him, truth process is an approach to peacebuilding that opens and washes political wounds, allowing us to see the nature of the toxic conditions those wounds have created and to begin to heal the poison of injustice and oppression. Then, when the wounds are healing, the balm of reconciliation can be applied. In the post-Apartheid period, Tutu urged people to practice forgiveness to aid the social healing process; he eventually wrote a book recounting his experiences and insights, *No Future without Forgiveness*.

Archbishop Tutu understood the complexity of the search for truth and the way it can lock us inside the victim/perpetrator polarity. His is a truth worthy of bearing witness to: "Having looked the beast of the past in the eyes, having asked and received forgiveness, let us shut the door of the past, not to forget it, but to allow it not to imprison us."

Truth process also played a major role in the remarkable journey that Rwanda took to restore civil society and rebuild social cohesion after the genocide in 1994, which primarily targeted Tutsis and left eight hundred thousand dead. At the turn of the new millennium, the Rwandan government beefed up the indigenous village court system to engage people across the nation in local truth-recovery work and, where possible, to help reintegrate people who were involved in the genocide but not as its primary instigators. The Gacaca courts, as they are called, did an extraordinary job of engaging whole communities in re-creating precise details of crimes and culpability. They also gave an opportunity for perpetrators to express remorse. More than eighty thousand were processed through these people's courts. I was permitted by the government to observe a Gacaca trial, and what inspired me was the passionate engagement and determination of the community to establish the truth. In a Gacaca trial, everyone is allowed to speak and to ask questions—what a radical idea! When afforded opportunities like this, people in many cultures, particularly indigenous ones, are less oriented toward vengeance than we would think.

I remember vividly the sense of excitement I witnessed in the schoolhouse outside Kigali where the Gacaca trial was held. Five respected members of the community where the incident had occurred constituted the panel of judges. In a Gacaca court, any member of the community can raise a hand and be recognized to ask a question or make a comment. There is a palpable sense that the search for truth is a collective task. At times waves of intense attention gripped the packed schoolhouse as people saw holes in the testimony or recognized a dramatic confirmation of events. The Gacaca is not just about documenting the facts for posterity but also about assessing the genuine cooperation of defendants in clarifying details and expressing remorse. When a community participates in uncovering the truth and assessing the cooperation of the perpetrator, people experience a degree of emotional catharsis. The Gacaca gives people an opportunity to participate in the justice system in a way that sets the stage for reconciliation more than heavy punishment would.

Cultures that emphasize collective rights, such as Rwanda's, often tend to appreciate that there is some degree of collective responsibility for crimes committed by individuals. Cultures that emphasize individual rights, like those in the West, tend to exact punishment on individuals and minimize the relevance of social conditions and the cohesion of communities. I believe justice will serve truth—and truth, justice—when we spend less time singling people out for punishment and more time on creating healthier familial, communal, and social environments. Both South Africa and Rwanda have set a high benchmark for how we can both seek facts and process collective experience after periods of intense human rights violations and trauma.

Honoring the truth of experience

In the twentieth century, physicists made an interesting discovery. They found that there is no neat dividing line between human consciousness and the subatomic substrate of matter. Previously, it was believed that a solid divide separated subject and object, mind and matter. But the exploration of the subatomic realm led these scientists to assert the existence of an observer effect: that observers interact with what they observe and collapse the field of the potential behaviors of the subatomic realm into either a wave or a particle function. Consciousness is somehow mysteriously entangled with matter.[3]

At roughly the same time, scientists in other fields were beginning to see there was no clear-cut distinction between mind and body: mind was seen to be distributed throughout the body as what pharmacologist Candace Pert calls "the molecules of emotion." We have also come to see that the heart acts more like a brain than a mechanical pump and that even our attitudes are implicated in turning our genetic switches on or off. Now, we cannot think about well-being without framing it in the context of mind-body health.

These and other important trends in the twentieth century brought back the quest to integrate human experience into our maps of reality rather than relegating subjective experience to some status below that of pure objective reason. In fact, we began to see the emergence of integral maps based on deepening conversations between spiritual practitioners and the scientific community. In sum, not only was human experience given greater credence and validity but also consciousness itself was elevated to a new level of significance.

But sharing experience is not an invitation for "anything goes." After spending over fifteen years in dialogue work, I would like to offer some pointers on how to share deep experience in meaningful ways:

1. Recognize the difference between experience and mental frameworks

There is a distinct difference between sharing what happened to you—and sharing the emotional impact those events had on you—and what you believe about the causes of those events in the larger scheme of things. People can say a lot of inflammatory and ungrounded things that issue from inherited beliefs, conditioned attitudes, and mental maps. Prejudice and stereotypes feed off mental imagery that is shared as fact: "If they had a chance they would wipe us all out." "They are all terrorists—they follow Islam."

But a person's account of an actual experience can be in marked contrast to these mental frameworks. Our goal as peacebuilders is to lead people to insights like this: "I know terrible things have been done, but I haven't been exposed to that personally. In fact, my neighbor and I get along, and he is a decent person." So the skillful peacebuilding work here is to help elicit people's direct experience and to have them reflect on those facts in the relative absence of interpretive layers. This means that you are not interacting at the level of assessing the accuracy or inaccuracy of a belief, or your agreement or lack of agreement about that belief, but that you are genuinely interested in having someone share the naked experience, detail by detail. In each case, eliciting a narration of the person's concrete experience will lead you to truth in ways that attitude and opinion cannot.

2. Do not challenge anyone's experience

Experience is sacred territory, and if you treat it as such, you will make progress in cultivating peace. It is not your work to determine if someone's experience has validity or not. Always show reverence for the act of sharing an experience. Nothing helps us bond more deeply than to access the truth of a person's experience and for that person to feel seen and heard without judgment. Challenging a person's experience from your own mental frameworks can trigger, traumatize, or leave the other feeling that the truth itself is being questioned. If you have been able to separate out mental models and belief structures so as to home in on the experience, do not then become reductionist or dismissive about the nature of that experience or seek to cast blame.

3. Do not create hierarchies of experience

Sometimes we can inadvertently minimize another person's experience by trying to contextualize it in relationship to more difficult experiences. Avoid this tendency. It is one thing for people to compare their own experience to others'; it is quite another for you to attempt to do that for them. Allow people to share their experience in ways that free them up to describe the emotional intensity they felt in the moment. Sometimes we devalue our own and others' experiences by framing them in ways that suggest a hierarchy of victimhood.

What we are looking for are the qualities and feeling tones of the experience, and we allow people to speak for themselves. I was in a group dialogue where a man who had survived genocide was speaking with a woman who had lost her son to AIDS. She described receiving a call from the police that her son had been found running naked and demented through the streets of Santa Barbara. We felt the deep pain of a mother watching her son die in this terrible way. The genocide survivor described being forced to play his flute as a ten-year-old boy as the Khmer Rouge butchered people in front of him. What was so moving was the way they shared: without any sense of trying to establish who had suffered more but instead with an understanding of how deeply each had experienced very different kinds of trauma. There are indeed extremes of pain and suffering, but what humanizes us is to know that we are not isolated in our suffering and that people can relate to whatever it is we have experienced.

4. Explore what people's experiences mean to them

Although you are not permitted to question the accuracy of people's experiences, it is helpful to sensitively explore with them what meaning their experiences have for them. What is significant in this regard is that we can guide others to change their relationship to the pivotal experiences in their lives, revealing quite new and different meanings. When exploring the meaning of an experience with someone, we should do our best to avoid asking leading questions that might imply that a better or more desired meaning can be derived. Trust that an empathic, open, and neutral form of questioning will elicit more truth than one that is creating a subterraneous passage to the right answer.

Be prepared to be deeply surprised when people draw powerfully affirmative meanings out of deeply negative experiences. So many people I have met on this journey have shared how they have evolved and grown. It is not that they would wish their suffering upon themselves or anyone else but that somehow their suffering became a doorway for an expanded life purpose. Such was the case of a man I met in Northern Ireland who was blinded as a boy by being shot by a British soldier at close range with a rubber bullet. He acknowledged how powerful he became as a voice for justice, healing, and reconciliation as a result of his experience. In a way that may be hard to understand, he had deep gratitude for his life as it was.

5. Help identify displaced emotion masquerading as experience

Once you have tuned in to people's narrations of events as directly experienced by them, you learn to decipher those parts of their stories coming from beliefs and mental models and those coming from the displaced feelings of resentment or hurt. Helping people locate the real source of their anger, wounding, and hostility is tremendously valuable in guiding them toward what is true within themselves. Therapists are trained in this arena, and it does require both psychological insight and skill to cautiously examine with another person where the feelings are really coming from. We know that we have a tendency to project onto others what we have failed to resolve in ourselves.

Again, leading questions will generally backfire. You have to be an ally of the other person in the effort to rediscover the actual experience, not a missionary pursuing the truth that you have determined is the only truth. The truth, when located in the place where it really resides, not where it has been displaced, is invariably more raw, original, and surprising than we would have imagined. When we encounter this lived truth, no matter how terrible or painful it is, its rootedness in reality activates the person; it comes into aliveness from the partial death of being covered over. If you have helped someone locate the real source of his or her pain and anger, it is truly a sacred experience in itself. The wonderful aspect of the mysterious and sacred encounter with another's experience is that you do not know how it will transform either you or them.

6. Recognize the great value in sharing experiences in circle

I have witnessed countless occasions when people have shared their experiences in circle formats where trust and confidentiality were established. In my life, very few things are more sacred. Well-conceived and carefully organized encounters where people share their life stories and their own journeys with wounding and healing can bring peace at a great depth. Building a field of trust together liberates the truth and allows us to look in the mirror of other people's experience and to see ourselves more clearly.

I have sat in dialogue with people who were tortured, who were combatants, who were forced to kill as children, who were sexually exploited and abused from an early age, who were exposed to racism, and who in the process overcame deep hatred. In so many cases, hearing someone else's experience gave them the courage to tell their own story from the inside out. We have a profound capacity to hear the ring of truth when people share how they were affected rather than merely giving us a linear accounting of the facts of what happened. It is this sound of truth that has the power to heal like no other sound on earth.

I was asked to submit a statement for an upcoming book titled *How Do You Pray?* This is what I submitted, which attests to my belief in the power of the truth that arises from sharing deep experience in circle:

A Rwandan woman sits in a circle telling her story of great family loss in the genocide. She is overcome with tears. Words fail. Her grief pulls her to lie face down on the ground. An African American woman who has dedicated her life to racial healing comes and lies down on the floor beside her, also face down. Then a third woman who has given most of her life to working with children of war and others who have endured great trauma also lies down beside her. The spirits of so much hurt and wounding crowd around the three prostrate women. A Hopi elder, a grandmother, rises and prays over them with simple dignity. Light enters the story.

This is how I pray in circle after circle. I offer my heart's capacity to open. I allow the molten lava of suffering to flow through it. Then when it is ready, in silence, in stillness, this heart becomes witness to the incomparable beauty of healing. And everything within me becomes a song.

Committing to a vision of peace

It is important to enter into a relationship with one's vision of peace, for it often contains a hologram of a greater truth. Cultivating peace requires cultivating vision. Without vision our experience of truth will be piecemeal. On the other hand, no one can put everything together. You are not being asked to do that. What you are asked to do is experience some concentrated power of vision to guide and sustain you. Vision is holographic. It shows us the whole in the part; it gives us the essence without a lot of details. When vision reveals itself, it does not come with a tactical A to Z of how to accomplish it. Vision calls for dynamic engagement. Vision is to be interacted with so that it pulls from us our truest and deepest qualities and capacities. Getting a vision and living it are two different things. Both are required.

Vision does its part by helping ignite passion, imagination, and spiritual calling. We do our part by becoming intimately committed to the vision. Great scientists, reformers, and social innovators know that a profound imaginative engagement with one's vision is necessary. One has to experience the template of its wholeness.

One thing we see clearly in the lives of people such as Susan B. Anthony, Mohandas Gandhi, Nelson Mandela, Aung San Suu Kyi, William Wilberforce, and great poets, artists, and inventors is this sense of lifelong communion with a deeply held vision. But faithfulness to the vision is invariably tested. To become actualized, the wholeness of the vision needs sustained interaction with a unique creativity.

Part of that testing (and the catalyst for unusual creativity) comes from the interests that feel threatened by our vision. By meeting the counterforce, in whatever form it takes, the visionary is creatively challenged to manifest an aspect of the vision. We are pulled out of the ivory tower of abstractions into the flesh-and-blood reality of incarnating the vision in time and space. Neuroscientists agree that human creativity invariably arises from the energy invested in meeting fresh challenges: we literally tune up our neural circuitry by attempting to manifest our vision in the face of difficulty or crisis. Here is where our strategies and tactics are constantly changed by the reality of conditions on the ground. But if we live inside a heartfelt vision, it will reenergize us to find another path to our goal. If the effectiveness of a singular strategy determines whether we win or lose, we may find ourselves burned out or depressed when it doesn't deliver what we need. When that happens, we must go back again and again to the hologram of the whole contained in the vision; our gold lies there—not in our tactics or strategies.

It is in this sense that peace is not for the faint of heart or the timid of vision or for those who fixate on particular approaches.

True vision points to a much higher integration of truth than the dominant modus operandi that it offers to replace; a compelling vision provides the energy of living inside a genuine evolutionary solution that motivates us to do what seems impossible. If instead we stare into the whirlpools of entropy where an overwrought focus on problems drains our energy, the very scale of our problems can hypnotize and paralyze us. This is where every form of linear objection arises to challenge the integrity of our vision: "But you haven't raised enough money." "You don't have the skills." "Why should they listen to you?" The limited view assaults the whole, and visionary truth is asked to surrender to small-time profit or myopic advantage. This kind of energy always seeks to drain vision because it simply cannot see up to the level of the visionary solution. What it cannot see, it does not know.

As a peace ambassador, you learn that you do not keep telling people what they do not know; you must instead find ways to give them a taste of what you can know together. This model of organizing is about *presence* and *being*, not just about communicating a compelling idea.

One thing should be clear to you by now: the emerging paradigm of peace work does not declare its truth by seeking out heathen warmongers and converting them. It is a radical commitment to co-experiencing a truth that does not objectify others or their truth perspectives but always places as its goal relational communing and the growth of mutual understanding through dialogue and true listening, new contexts for social emergence, and even truth process.

Vision accompanied by this kind of commitment is what keeps us from the energy that drains and what leads us to the energy that replenishes and sustains. It is nothing less than the truth of an evolving future calling us to manifest its purpose and perfection.

THE
Call

It is good to remember Albert Einstein's advice: "Whoever undertakes to set himself up as a judge of Truth is shipwrecked by the laughter of the gods." Truth, or what powerful interests hold as "the truth," has often been wielded as a weapon and as a clarion call to castigate others and even as the justification for violence. In order for such partial truth to work in this way, it has to constantly focus on exclusions. If you are going to bludgeon someone with the truth, you will need a blunt instrument and not one whose edges are compromised by subtleties and nuances. But you, as a peace ambassador, are called upon to be the voice of all those gray areas in the exclusion zone of those who want to manipulate our attention or have us imagine a simplistic polarity of moral choices.

Be the voice of courageous nuance and great subtlety.

Truth has been made into a marketable commodity, and merchants of this kind of packaged truth will tell you that you either have it or you don't. You can be conned into believing that truth always takes sides, always dividing those who are for it from those who are against it. Those who feel called to be crusaders or vigilantes of truth are ceaselessly looking for its enemies. But take a closer look, and you will see that what they are protecting is a very partial truth, a carefully fortified niche of the truth. But you are called to represent truth as a vivid and faithful exploration of the reality we *all* find ourselves living in.

You are called to investigate, explore, and seek out the many faces of truth. And you are challenged to bring forth a vision of how the many can find a higher truth that is both coherent and unifying. Never make your slice of the truth a wedge that divides.

You have come to know that the processes we engage to discover truth tell us how deeply we are looking for it. Be the guardian of truth process more than the messenger of truth claims. Know that opening to a true democratic process will provoke those with vested interests: this is where you need fierce courage and great wisdom to stay heart centered when encountering those bent on poisoning the well of good process.

Linear facts have their importance and relevance, and we cannot expect to find a deeper truth if we deny them. Tampering with the facts is an indicator of deceitful motivation. Human rights groups do well to constantly demand a true and accurate accounting of all levels of involvement in violations: the truth requires that we understand command structures and not just accountability. But just getting such facts can cost lives. Thank God for the investigative journalists, NGOs, and news organizations, like Al Jazeera, that are interested in deeper human rights reporting. Finding reliable sources of information from multiple sources is essential for informed peace work.

Peace requires that we know who is trying to subvert it and why. Be a voice for a media that gives us more than catastrophe headlines. Stop consuming media that is nothing more than the voice of corporate worldviews, entrenched in covering peevish distractions.

Demand that the media you consume go deeper and deeper into the causal weave of violence. It is one thing to track down the accountability of those who ordered and perpetrated crimes and abuses; it is another to understand the conditions that fostered those problems and how those conditions were allowed to flourish. As a twenty-first-century ambassador of peace you must do more than skim the surface of truth if you are to be effective. Go to the root of *belief systems* that carry outmoded codes of inequity, that tolerate prejudice, that despoil nature, and that breed dominance and unhealthy competition.

Become both a high practitioner of dialogue and an articulate spokesperson for a larger, more inclusive vision. Dialogue allows for space between conflicting facts and subjective truths so that something new can be heard, something that offers an evolving synthesis and the possibility of a new consensus.

Vision holds the templates of wholeness, and without it we harden our conviction that our perspective is the only true and viable one. Constantly feed and renew yourself from a living vision. If your vision is too small, you will be defeated by all kinds of linear obstruction; if it is too grandiose, you will self-destruct.

As we have noted earlier, you are also called upon to release the wounds of the past, since they become a regressive influence on the emergence of new social truth. Until the wounds of the past are resolved and healed, they will create so much entropy that people will keep spinning around old problems and outmoded political fixations.

We live in an age of media cacophony where news is entertainment and opinion is confused with fact. Yet increasingly people are exchanging the kind of information that really matters to them. We have new tools that provide us with the means to share our truth, explore our questions, find kindred spirits, build like-minded communities, and participate in dialogue and debate with people who differ. Without a doubt this social ferment is seriously competing with official and corporate information channels and is giving us a more reliably democratic take on what is unfolding around us. Never has the opportunity to participate in shaping the nature and quality of collective attention been greater. Be the voice of the emerging media narrative through social networking, so that your own deeper and more nuanced voice of truth is heard.

Yet avoid offerings that are not grounded in a more rigorous truth process and experiential validation. It is essential that our truth as peacebuilders not be a sound bite, a marketing tactic, a mere aspiration, or a collection of disembodied ideas. Our truth must have the authentic seal of lived experience and practiced commitment.

Our most evolved relationship to truth, as beings committed to peace, goes to the heart of our passion and convictions without feeding off energy that deems other people wrong. Admittedly, many people cannot even see that this is possible, and they think, "If I am right about this, you must be wrong." It is imperative in peace work that we understand why this limited truth formula is so conducive to hostility, particularly when it is part of a group psyche or when the subject inflames people's passions.

Speak your truth boldly, resolutely, and with deep conviction. Please do not relegate peace work to some kind of inauthentic niceness and emotional flatness. We evolve because people speak new truths with visionary clarity and moral courage and with their own unique communicative style and flair. There is no sense that we should not highly honor audacity or bold originality.

Again, we are collectively called upon to go beyond any form of zealotry that makes others wrong. We must do our utmost to affirm and deepen the ground of being with others, even as we go toe to toe over ideological, theological, or philosophical differences. That is how we participate in an evolutionary leap forward.

Remember that the ground of being is always nurtured by respect. This is not some mental attitude that tells you to keep your animosity in abeyance; it is a deep sensorial contact with another's being. Aqeela Sherrills, who helped make peace between rival gangs in Los Angeles, says it is even deeper than respect; it is about cultivating reverence for others—for all beings. Be a part of the reverence movement.

Naturally, in some circumstances all you can do is refrain from reciprocating inflammatory and threatening behaviors. But this peaceful stance at least shows that you honor the person while disagreeing with their ideas. With advanced practice you can deepen the circuitry of connection with others, even as you diverge with them over big questions. This is where we all need to evolve our capacity to create a tidal wave of change in how we human beings do business with one another.

It is a profound error to confuse a person with the ideas he or she holds. When we do so, we generally sacrifice greater truths for lesser ones. We sacrifice the truth of what we have in common for the truth of what we differ about. Demagogues, and there are plenty of petty, fiercely negative ones around, make a profession out of assaulting the dignity of others over differences. The media loves to cover these vulgar and opportunist displays of confected conflict, but peacebuilders do the opposite. They skillfully affirm what instigators of violence deny: that we are one in the spirit and that if we work hard enough we will experience our unity long before most of our theologians and politicians catch up with it.

Peace is not possible without an experience of unity, and unity cannot be experienced without full permission for diversity and plurality to thrive. This is the truth that sets us free to be both who we are as creative individuals, as diverse cultures, and as an emerging planetary civilization, with a responsibility for harmonious and sustainable life on earth. Yes, we are now collectively ready for the advanced class in deep democracy, conscious evolution, and spiritual development. So show us now how *you* do your dance with this truth!

Reflection AND Practice

All of this suggests that we need to evolve beyond our current capacities if we are to up-level our peace work and get out of the sandbox of who is right and who is wrong. Formulate and articulate a coherent and inclusive vision of peace that reflects visionary truth.

Practice speaking your truth from this vision and not reactively to others' viewpoints. Let your vision be a source and a reference point for your work; feel its aliveness and its contagiousness. Learn to contact it as a substance that holds nutrition. As you develop this practice, you will find you are less reactive or triggered by viewpoints that disturb you and even those that may be threatening. You may discover that you have been feeding off negative energy rather than the generative energy of your own vision.

This should facilitate another related practice: cultivate empathic connection and compassionate engagement so that you can receive and connect with the way other people speak their truth. Keep a warm sympathetic energy in your heart during a tense or conflicted encounter, and when you feel your adrenaline beginning to spike, quietly breathe more slowly and deeply into your heart. Your aim is to become more adept at tuning in to when and how other people speak their truth. Once you can focus on that, you will be better able to build that field of resonance discussed in chapter 5. Once a person feels seen, you cross a barrier that helps truths engage. When a person feels not seen, that barrier only gets denser and more divisive.

Wherever possible, create a circle or other dialogic environment where people can safely share deep experiences and diverse viewpoints. There are many circle formats, but their one central concept is to demonstrate reverence for the truth of another person's experience. If you create a circle, make it clear that you want to learn from people's direct experience. Debating ideas or airing opinions can be done at another time.

Evaluate your media consumption patterns and your own participation in new media. Research and support human rights data collection, investigative journalism, and initiatives that apply deep analysis to reveal the root causes of systemic injustices. Part of being a peace ambassador is honing your own capacity to represent truth in your society. How tenaciously or creatively are you speaking out on pivotal peace and social justice issues? Do a little inventory and see where your voice is being made visible and where you remain more passive. You have your own way of seeking and expressing truth, but let it not be said that you remained silent during the most pivotal time in the planet's struggle to create models of ecological sustainability, economic justice, and enlightened global governance.

Getting at the truth is not just a matter of simply asking questions, is it? So often we ask positional questions rather than genuinely open ones. Let's face it: we can be sneaky and surreptitious inquisitors, out to reveal the wrongheadedness of others.

We create a kind of entrapment to prove, at least to ourselves, where others are wrong. We are so conditioned by the need to have the right answers that we can find that our internal process is structured around the reward felt for being in the right. What can appear on the surface as openness can often be a polite veneer hiding impatience with people who just don't get it. But truth is not an object, nor is it about scoring points. It is about how genuinely and authentically we can relate to each other or even commune together to experience the emergence of higher ground.

When that happens, we find ourselves leaving hardened and congealed dogmatic truths and moving into subtle truth processes where shades of meaning are explored and where there are breathing spaces for others' truth. Paradoxically, it is only then that we can ask the most daring, searching, and far-reaching questions of each other. Once the ground of being has been made safe, we can and must push each other to evolve toward even greater truth.

Carry with you a vision of this greater field where we human beings grow together and evolve into capacities that make us truly more loving and wise and where we experience the ultimate truth of our most profound connection to one another and all the responsibility that brings.

Chapter 7

~

Peaceful Communication
and Energy Mastery

Energy mastery for peacemakers is about learning to align awareness and higher consciousness with the body's intelligence and to tune in to its precise and subtle signals. I spent much of my earlier career ignoring those signals, feeling that the higher moral ground of peace and human rights activism entitled me to berate government officials who represented or supported abusive regimes. One member of Congress, feeling the heat of my ire, told me I reminded him of a Scottish Presbyterian minister. We can feel safe at the pulpit talking *at* bullies and their surrogates. We can expose them and guilt-trip them, but rarely can we transform them in this way. We can ride the high horse of moral superiority and even feel an adrenaline high when we boldly confront those in power who sell out in ways that increase human suffering, but in the end we have to get off that horse and tune in to the deeper voice of our own humanity. That deeper voice asks us to pay attention to the energy we are putting out into the world. In the end, self-righteousness is a seduction that stirs an energy of divisiveness. Our task as peace ambassadors is not to mute criticism but to cultivate that subtle energy which heals and does no harm.

Often to be a healing presence in a conflict situation we have to be both calm and effective in defusing highly volatile energy. Peacemakers have to learn how to avoid becoming triggered themselves, or they will end up adding fuel to the fire because they can't handle the energy of confrontation. When they master the energy of their own fight-or-flight response, they not only help prevent violence but also can help initiate a transition from bare-knuckled hostility to dialogue. Even in a matter of minutes, as the energy of rage gathers momentum, a situation can sometimes be transformed by a much subtler nonthreatening energy.

Before we examine this aspect of energy mastery and peacemaking, let's explore some contemporary thinking about energy. Whether solid, liquid, or gas, the deepest substrate of everything is energy. Even thoughts and emotions have an energetic component. The body has its own electromagnetic energy field. The heart has a field five thousand times as strong as the electrical charge of the brain. Different energy frequencies in the brain bring us into contrasting states of consciousness: at 0.5 to 4.0 Hertz we are in a delta state and asleep; at 4.0 to 7.5 Hz we are in theta, drifting from sleep to vision states and intuitive perception; in the alpha state, from 7.5 to 13 Hz, we experience deep, calm listening, relaxation, meditation, and peaceful intention; the beta state comprises 14 to 40 Hz and includes athletic activity and all forms of sharply alert, focused, and aroused attention.

We have come to know that subtle energy not only exists but also is increasingly integrated into various health practices and healing modalities. For example, Reiki has gained increased respect as an energy-healing approach that does not even involve any physical massage or touching. Johrei, a similar practice, which, like Reiki, originated in Japan, is connected to spiritual intention and is used as a daily practice among some family members. More people in the West are picking up Eastern energy practices derived from the martial arts, such as qigong and tai chi. The Chinese concept of *chi*, like the Indian idea of *prana*, refers to subtle or vital energy that we can activate to improve our health and overall well-being.

We are indeed creatures designed to register subtle energetic shifts: we are capable of feeling gradual and hardly detectable changes in our own moods, and if we are keenly attuned, we can pick up these same mood shifts in others. The body is an antenna that is alert to dangers, threats, and opportunities in the world around it. This extends into the world of meaning, where it can equally pick up the energetic signals associated with love, respect, appreciation, and camaraderie, as well as signals of dislike, arrogance, superiority, and hostility. The brain processes scores of signals simultaneously with its capacity for conscious awareness, but many thousands of inputs are deciphered off the radar screen of the conscious mind in the spacious underworld of the subconscious.

To be effective at peace work, one must go far beyond merely dealing with spoken input. Ambassadors of peace must also become highly skillful in perceiving energetic shifts and signals in themselves and in others. This work can be compared to aikido, a martial art that skillfully uses the energy of an opponent for mutual protection. Its founder, Morihei Ueshiba, insisted that it had its base in moral principles, peace, and harmony.

Like an aikido master, the representative of peace learns to see energy as it forms and to embrace its life force instead of becoming a distorted mirror of its threat or anger. Mastery in peacebuilding requires that we care so deeply for others that we do not use our unskillful behavior against them. Peaceworkers make sure they do no harm to themselves or anyone else. In this practice, we become adept at seeing how intention creates a pattern of energetic movement: if you are able to read or anticipate people's intentions, you will be able to address the root cause of their energy as it accelerates from its source and will therefore know its trajectory in the world of effects. In essence, your intention must always be to both protect yourself and others while you also protect your attackers and by skillful means reveal to them a path to their higher nature, where worthy intentions manifest harmonious effects.

The skillful management and liberation of energy aligned with the clearest intention to cultivate peace is an important aspect of the curriculum for anyone who wants to work for reconciliation and healing. We human beings are energy processers, and by that I mean not just physical energy but also the complex interaction of thoughts, feelings, and moods that are reflected in the whole continuum of the mind and body. The body alerts us when the ideas, attitudes, or behaviors of others trigger us. When we feel rejected or judged, the body registers threat just as much as it produces hormonal pleasure signals when we are admired and appreciated. Cultivating awareness about this inner flow and being able to witness our own reactivity is the first step in developing the necessary mastery of our energy as peacemakers. By gaining this inner mastery, the peacemaker can make sure the blood doesn't "boil over" in ways that hurt or humiliate others. More than that, truly effective ambassadors of peace will do more than center themselves in the storm of volatile energy; as noted, they will help transform the unskillful aggression of others. Peacemakers who can align both conscious intention and a high motivation to be peaceful human beings with an ability to defuse hostile and reactive energy in themselves and others are worthy of being called twenty-first-century ambassadors of peace.

The aikido of dealing with bullies

Bullying has three energy conduits: physical, emotional, and intellectual. In this section, I offer my understanding of how people manage their energy to bully others and how we can respond.

The physical bully
Whether or not they use their physical prowess to actually beat up others, physical bullies use their bodies to dominate. In fact, physical bullies have a way of consciously or unconsciously using the body to create alpha dominance—an impression that they are the most powerful presence in the room. We are all familiar with the swagger associated with this aggressive form of physicality. We often experience in

the presence of a physical bully an invasion of our personal space, an unwillingness or inability to read the subtle cues of others, and constant signals or allusions to physical strength. Contrary to the stereotype, I do not believe this type is typically a good athlete, since athletes are always conscious of their physical strengths and weaknesses and are more perceptively attuned to their bodies and those of others.

Think back to the schoolyard, and it probably won't be difficult to identify the physical bullies. We can recall a certain quality of anger they carried around, whether or not they were menacing others or picking on "weaker" kids. Depending on the intensity of their rage, they found ways to make others look smaller: flipping someone's hat, pushing, pinching, or punching.

Physical bullies use the only vehicle open to them in attempting to power up their energy dominance. If you can remember such people from your childhood, you may recall that they couldn't handle emotional nuance or complexity and were threatened by those who could outwit them intellectually. In other words, they were often emotionally blocked as a result of being emotionally wounded and were afraid that they would lose their strength if people recognized the nature of the wound. Or they were afraid of being laughed at or looking dumb because they felt intellectually inferior. Or they were emotionally locked in for other reasons, such as cultural machismo or homophobia.

The aikido for these bullies is to be physically relaxed in their presence, thereby presenting a kind of neutralizing energy in response to their display of physical energy dominance; the last thing you want is to seem overly submissive or fearful or to get into a "display of power" contest. Next, you want to demonstrate attunement to their emotions or to any ideas they have. You care for such people by skillfully giving credence to their right to have their emotions and their intellect understood and accepted. Give them respect and try to coach them into expressing feelings and ideas. Respect does not require agreement, but it does require attunement. You focus on where the energy is locked, not on the way it is spilling over. When it is spilling over in a particularly unskillful way, commenting on the spillage does no good and usually exacerbates the problem. Follow the trajectory of the energy back to its source and offer support there.

Men who become physically violent, who beat and abuse women, and who demonstrate unwanted sexual aggression need therapy. It is one thing to defuse a highly explosive situation; it is another to deal with the underlying causes. We need to see bullying as a family and community health issue and deal with it as such before it becomes a serious crime. Even then, an enlightened criminal justice system will address pathology with specific therapeutic treatments and not exacerbate it with alpha-dominated prison violence.

One inspired group that deals creatively with school bullying and helps nip it in the bud is Challenge Day, founded by two educators in Northern California. The Challenge Day mission is to provide youth and their communities with programs that demonstrate the possibility of love and connection through the celebration of diversity, truth, and full expression: "where bullying, violence and other forms of oppression are a thing of the past."[1] As noted author and social activist Riane Eisler and many other evolved leaders have pointed out, we must deal with the cultural roots of male domination, the conditioned fixations about power transmitted to young men, and the structures of hierarchical oppression that male aggression creates in society. Our educational systems must do this primary peace work to address the roots of physical aggression, as well as other forms of bullying.

The emotional bully

The emotional bully has learned that emotional intimidation can be used as effectively as physical threat to control, manipulate, or coerce others. Emotional bullying can range from explicit threats to subtle insinuations. Emotional bullies develop an ability to see other people's vulnerabilities. They study vulnerability so that they can master it to their advantage. Emotional bullying is skillful at triggering guilt, shame, embarrassment, self-doubt, fear, and a sense of inadequacy in others. It can be a blunt instrument of aggression or surgically precise (hence the idea of being "needled").

People can wake up to the fact that they have been in long-term relationships with emotional bullies as parents, siblings, spouses, or that they have succumbed to emotional bullying in the workplace. It can be difficult to unwind this form of bullying and even more difficult to deal with the emotional bullies themselves. Confronting them head-on, particularly in the midst of conflict, will invariably trigger an intensification of the bullying. It is like cornering an animal that must attack to survive.

The aikido here is to recognize the manipulation and not to respond to it. Sometimes silence is a perfect antidote. You are attempting not to confront the energetic distortion designed to needle, hurt, or bring you under the other person's control but to mirror nonviolently and nonreactively that you have witnessed the manipulation. This mirroring, which shows that you have not been baited, is extremely powerful. It helps the bullies see that you see what is going on. You are also making sure their fishing expeditions haven't hooked you. You must therefore be perceptive about how you get hooked and triggered, for after all, the bullies are trying to work your vulnerabilities. Here the representative of peace is helping emotional bullies gain insight into their own process of feeding off the energy of other people in a dysfunctional way. It is also important to model how to obtain healthy emotional reciprocity with other people, in ways that support other people's strengths rather than leeching off their vulnerabilities, so that the bullies can see how they can find the nurturing energy they so desperately need.

Remember that our emotional processing patterns begin early in life. Positive emotion is elixir for human beings, and when we cannot get our emotional needs met, we can become bandits hijacking others to secure the life-giving food of love and appreciation. What a tragedy it is when people play misers with their storehouse of affection because it was given to them only under manipulative conditions. In this case, the lesson for the peacemaker is to never steal from misers but to be generous so they may learn generosity. When you have applied the right balm as a quiet ambassador of peace, you will have the joy of helping Scrooge wake up to his true wealth.

The intellectual bully

The intellectual bully has lost contact with the emotions as a source of replenishment and affirmation. Instead, the ego takes over and uses the intellect to draw the energy of admiration and the rewards of success. Just as physical and emotional bullies seek to dominate their respective spaces, so do intellectual bullies. Displays of intellectual prowess are accompanied by aggression toward other viewpoints and theories. This form of bullying is dismissive and redolent of arrogance. It can be expressed in oh-so-subtle and sophisticated putdowns. It can be hyper-rational and prone to the use of exclusive terminology. It is oriented to in-group conversations and an inflated sense of self-appreciation for its own mental acrobatics. It knows how to skewer people from the safe towers of its superior vantage point but is out of reach of its own boiling emotional cauldron.

When the ego dominates the intellect, it is always competitive and incapable of appreciating true collaboration. Ego is driven by a hidden envy of those who gain recognition or who seem to thrive effortlessly; such envy is a deeply destructive force in society rarely acknowledged as violence.

The aikido for intellectual bullying is to abstain from gratifying the ego of those who indulge in it. Being willing to support such people without getting spun in the coils of their ego performance requires a capacity for holding a strong nonjudgmental presence. Simply dismissing pompous and arrogant people is no solution. Presence suggests that we are conscious, aware, and focused. We mirror a state of wholeness that reflects physical, emotional, and mental integration. This integrated presence provides a contrast to the intellectual bully's shrill or hollow displays of purely mental agility. We attempt to be an anchor so that the other person who is billowing in the mental realm can experience coming down into an emotional and physical center. Quietly focusing on your own heart, as well as the other person's, can amplify the vibration of deeper and more authentic communication.

Our educational system is responsible for fostering and rewarding intellectual competitiveness at the expense of more holistic approaches. The scientific research on emotional intelligence and social intelligence suggests that it is a grave error to leave them out of the school curriculum. It is time we educated for wholeness and for wisdom rather than cognitive dominance. Teachers can become ambassadors of peace who have a truly privileged role in nurturing a culture in which those who inherit our future are able to collaborate, empathize, and express the fullness of human wisdom.

If we are not careful, we shall all go down with the educated cleverness that has come to proliferate as so-called expert viewpoints or the callous aggression of so many well-paid pundits. As peace ambassadors dedicated to creating a culture of peace, we can offer a different evolutionary path—a path that eschews the cleverness and destructive nature of ego and that integrates a holistic mind-body awareness in service to genuine human advancement.

Processing energy in conflict situations

Another method of cultivating energy mastery in peace work is to recognize the four fundamental ways of processing energy in relationships, only one of which is transformative in the way it leads to inner peace and relational peace with others. A fuller background to this discussion can be found in my book *Creative Stress: A Path for Evolving Souls Living through Personal and Planetary Upheaval.*

The energy bouncer
In situations of conflict, people come across as energy bouncers when they disguise or attempt to disguise the fortress of defenses they have created to deal with any incoming energy. It is as if they have made their emotional world off limits. They are threatened by intimacy and deal swiftly with any perceived criticism. They tend toward being loud and even boisterous as a defense; if they don't like what is coming at them, they will send it back at double the velocity. They may resort to authoritarian stances, invoking hierarchy and privilege, and use sarcasm or any number of other defensive tactics to avoid being closely questioned or scrutinized.

All too many politicians regularly use energy bouncing to look tough. They stifle real debate and avoid sincere self-reflection and introspection. Eventually, in some form or another, people who live under the illusion that they can just bounce energy off their well-constructed defenses find that one day it all boomerangs back on them. If they are lucky, they discover they have deprived themselves of the feedback they need most. More than that, they will one day discover that they have deprived themselves of experiencing the healing salve of genuine friendship and intimacy. They have denied themselves the life-giving energy of reciprocity.

Peace activists tend to clash with energy bouncers who use alpha dominance strategies, particularly because energy bouncers turn the tables and make peace activists the problem. We are all too familiar with accusations that advocates of peace are "commie sympathizers" or "enemies of national security" or any number of other epithets used to silence, sideline, or threaten those who hold opposing values. This is why it is so important to create a culture of peace and to make sure that peace work isn't framed as simply an opposition to war. The great challenge here is to avoid having the terms of any conversation or debate be dictated by those who are interested only in pushing aside concerns that get in their way.

The energy sponge

The opposite of energy bouncers are energy sponges: instead of putting up impenetrable defenses, they leave the door open and allow almost any kind of energy to take up residence. They seem to make every situation about themselves. They can spend a lifetime in "Why is it always my fault?" and "No one appreciates me." They live in a constant state of victimization. They are often drowning in emotion. They become deeply attached to the energy freight dragging them down and begin to define themselves by all the energy they are no longer capable of skillfully processing. Like a sponge that needs to be squeezed so that it releases excess water, this kind of condition requires help in letting go, forgiving, and moving on. Energy sponges need help in strengthening their expression of personal power and will and in moving out of blame-shame cycles.

The peacemaker knows, as we discussed in chapter 4 on wounding and healing, that the victims' attachment to wounding can become a serious threat to peace prospects. The wound can become so much a part of the victims' identity that it is transmitted to the next generation and easily used as a motivation for hostility or revenge. That is why social healing work, with its focus on interrupting the intergenerational transmission of wounding, becomes an important dimension of peace work.

The energy zapper

Energy zappers know how to kill emotion. They are experts in numbing difficult or painful energies. They may deal with their depleted energy with artificial stimulants, or they may choose drugs and alcohol to obliterate their pain or loss. They separate themselves from the actual work of dealing with challenges and replace it with fantasy and distraction. They often lack maturity and the capacity to appreciate how pain and difficulty can be our teachers if we let them. In the extreme, when it comes to peace, people who process energy in this way can view the peace movement as a kind of escape or a cozy world in which they can take drugs and get high. Peace can become a fantasy world without pain or struggle. Search for Common Ground, a premier peace and conflict-resolution organization with offices in many of the world's conflict zones, points out that conflict in itself is neither positive nor negative; conflict is simply a fact of life. Peace cannot be achieved if we pretend that we can live in a conflict-free world. To work with energy zappers, we must help them discover natural highs and the rewards that are experienced from facing challenges. The energy zapper needs to be initiated by those who have real wisdom to share or by those who have taken the hard journey through delusion and fake thrills to come home to the miraculous nature of reality as it is.

The energy transformer

In contrast with the previous types, the energy transformer is able to process energy in healthy and productive ways. Energy transformation always involves creativity. Experiences are actively engaged, and both passivity and aggression are avoided. Peace workers are not superhuman; we are not asked to transform pathological hatred, violent attack, or extremes of demeaning hostility. Rather, our work as peace ambassador calls us to be discerning and courageous about what we can peacefully disarm and engage and what reactive energy we must transform within ourselves.

This mature human capacity arises out of an ability to recognize the nature of any energy coming at us. This ability is sometimes referred to as summoning our internal witness. The witness is not abstracted from what is happening and is not a disengaged observer. The witness is engaged in perceptive participation without being hooked or triggered by what is unfolding. You could say that the witness is itself transforming by perceiving the real nature of events. If we witness our own prejudice or predisposition to be judgmental in certain arenas, we begin to catch ourselves in the act. As we cultivate that witness, we grow in knowledge about how to choose a better path. The witness brings *a knowing through seeing* that helps dissolve ignorance.

As an accurate and mature witness to unfolding events, the energy transformer does not attempt to make sweet what is bitter. Pain is not blocked, excessively dwelt upon, or numbed—it is fully experienced. Raw energy is refined by being met and understood. Escapism and defensiveness are seen as lost opportunities for growth.

Self-development is a key motivation for energy transformers, as is increasing the capacity for effective service—for service to the world becomes a constant rewarding experience of transforming blocked energy. Joy becomes the gold of an alchemical process in which the peace ambassador learns how to meet challenges instead of avoiding them. Every obstacle on the path becomes a teacher in one's development.

A leading proponent of nonviolent communication once described being in the home of a young Hamas activist and having a conversation with members of the household. When the young man arrived, he was enraged to find an American in his house. In addition, the American was Jewish. This was a potentially dangerous situation. Standing in his own home, the Hamas supporter was confronted with the very image and archetype of the enemy. He was boiling with rage as he demanded to know why such a person had been allowed into the house. Using a nonviolent communication strategy, the American asked whether the man needed him to understand the role that Americans played in the difficulties facing the Palestinians. The answer was, of course, a predictable affirmation of the man's conviction that Americans were a big element in his oppression.

What happened in that interaction was skillful energy-transforming work that opened up dialogue rather than degenerating into violence. The American visitor stayed calm and did not get hooked by the assaultive energy that came at him. From that place, he attempted to locate the fundamental need of the other to be seen, heard, and understood. By this act, he became an energy transformer in the teeth of a dangerous encounter. The nonviolent communication approach exemplified in this case was created by the master teacher and practitioner Marshall Rosenberg.[2] It was Rosenberg himself who was the American in that home.

Because they have learned how to transform charged, threatening, and hostile energy, peace activists can literally place themselves inside the cauldron of dangerous conflict zones. Take the work of Nonviolent Peaceforce, an international agency whose mission is to send unarmed civilians into areas of conflict to be a buffer and intermediary between opposing factions. Here's how the organization describes its work. As you read, reflect on how you might prepare yourself to deal with the energy extremes of tension and fear:

> We most often respond to invitations by credible local organizations committed to nonviolent solutions. Once invited, we meet key players, including commanders from opposing sides, local police, religious, business, and civil society leaders. We live and work in communities within conflict zones alongside local people.

When violence erupts, civilians under threat often contact us. They know and trust us. We have been living among them. Visibly nonpartisan and unarmed, we arrive in NP [Nonviolent Peaceforce] uniforms, with NP vehicles, letting our presence be known.

We build the confidence and safety of civilians deeply affected by conflict so they can access available structures and mechanisms for addressing problems and grievances.

Our activities have ranged from entering active conflict zones to remove civilians in the crossfire to providing opposing factions a safe space to negotiate. Other activities include serving as a communication link between warring factions, securing safe temporary housing for civilians displaced by war, providing violence prevention measures during elections, and negotiating the return of kidnapped family members.[3]

The core of energy transformation is not letting resentment, fear, or anger get stuck inside us. Sometimes we hold a resentment for a lifetime. The energy gets coiled in our musculature and shows up as constriction in our jaws, stiffness in the neck, and backache. It can show up as heightened blood pressure or as digestive problems. It can embed itself as an eating disorder, depression, or anxiety, or it can burst out over trivial matters. Energy transformers do not allow energy to stick to them; they deal with it in the moment instead of trying to push it away or swallow it. Energy is always on a journey: rocks become soil; soil becomes life-supporting nutrients; biochemical nutrients transform caterpillars into butterflies. And we humans constantly grow and evolve. As we evolve, we learn how to transmute denser energy into subtler energy: the tantrum of the child demanding attention transforms into the subtle exchanges of adult intercourse; the bullying demands of the dominator must eventually succumb to the power of reciprocity. To stop energy from hardening into psychological fixation and emotional attachment—and then into conflict and war—we must release it. We have seen that it cannot be released by venting or wallowing in a sense of victimization. So let's explore releasing energy in more depth.

Transforming energy through release

In order to achieve peace, we need to release blocked energy. Whether it's at the personal, familial, communal, or societal level, the principle holds true: what we don't release will eventually come back to hurt or haunt us.

Following the thread of teachings in the world's wisdom traditions, Everett Worthington and other scholars look at forgiveness as a form of letting go of harmful energy states. In his writings, Worthington talks about releasing the state of unforgiveness. The cauldron of anger, resentment, and desire for revenge, if not released, becomes toxic. It so happened that Worthington had a devastating experience that tested this belief: an assailant broke into his mother's home and bludgeoned her to death.

He had to allow himself the anger, pain, and grief that such an incident can provoke. But he knew that the intense pain and fury needed to be released. He did not forgive the deed, but he released all animosity and hostility toward the man who had carried it out. What Worthington did is sometimes referred to as catharsis: the purging of a deep toxin and its associated energies.[4]

Catharsis can come in many forms. The ancient Greek philosopher Aristotle built on the notion of medical purging to give us our contemporary sense of releasing pent-up emotions. He felt that audiences watching a tragedy could release their own subconscious fears or other emotions that might otherwise negatively control them if held on to.

Indeed, I have seen profound catharsis expressed through the arts. On a visit to Northern Ireland in 2009, I saw a performance by the Theater of Witness about the conflict there. The performers were real combatants and real victims of the violence. They told their stories and let them be a mirror for the audience. I was able to experience the truth of each side of the conflict as a complex equation rather than a neat version of good guys versus bad guys. Although I had known many of the facts and historical narratives, I had not experienced them in this way before. The intensity was palpable throughout the theater. The fact that audience members were allowed to ask questions and to share their own emotional process only added to the cathartic nature of the experience.

Sitting beside me during the performance was my colleague Judith Thompson. She and I had convened numerous social healing dialogues over the years aimed at helping people from the world's conflict zones to experience the deepest release of painful trauma. In many ways, these survivors of extreme cruelty and oppression were, and remain, our teachers of energy mastery. For ultimately there is no greater mastery than to transform the cauldron of severe wounding and humiliation into compassion for self and others.

It is also good to remind ourselves that healing catharsis can come from laughter as well as tears. Both are conduits of releasing pent-up energy. Laughter releases the pressure valve of internalized negative energy and can allow us to see a situation with fresh eyes unclouded by blocked feelings. Comedians can do more for peacebuilding than many a preacher.

We can also purge the trapped energy of guilt by acts of atonement. I recently wrote an essay on this subject titled "Creative Atonement in a Time of Peril," which appeared in the book *Beyond Forgiveness: Reflections on Atonement*.[5] The essay encourages us to creatively explore actions that will demonstrate our willingness to engage in repairing the damage done by unskillful actions in the past. Atonement is not about sackcloth and ashes; it is about releasing the wounds of the past in ways that transform resentment. In the essay, I tell the story of a soldier who, on breaking into a house in pursuit of the enemy, is confronted by the energy of hatred in the eyes of three children who stand and stare at him. In that moment, he has an epiphany: there can be no end to the conflict when such vivid hatred has already entered the hearts of young children. This soldier quickly left the military and now plays the flute and didgeridoo in schools. His actions did not transform the conflict, but they transformed him and many of the children he meets. He understood that to create a culture of peace we must not only release trapped negative energy but also release our deepest qualities and gifts to the world.

Getting to the root energy of qualities and gifts that have been blocked by guilt, fear, manipulation, distraction, or paralysis is one of the goals of this work. We have to learn to give expression to who it is we really are and slough off the numbed-down or dumbed-down version of ourselves. So much of our potential is not released. Imagine the degree of planetary transformation that would take place if all people could live their true potential. Now we have a key to a new kind of peace movement—one that sees its function as unlocking humanity's potential. Peace invites us to come out of hiding and to remember not only that it is safe to be ourselves but also that it is essential to express our gifts if we are to thrive.

Peace is flattened if it is formulated in a way that requires us to tamp down our uniqueness or to tone down the vibrancy of our passion. Energy mastery comes from being able to read those energies that, however tentatively, are moving toward resonance with others and those energies that want to mute any incipient harmonic.

We are actually leaking signals all over the place, both consciously and unconsciously. If lie detectors and other technological devices can pick up subtle information, do you really think humans cannot? Or maybe we want to believe that we cannot develop those capacities because we fear that people will see what we are thinking and feeling.

When you are able to read energy, you can be both more compassionate and more deft in dealing with others. You will find that you will know when to adroitly move aside because the energy that is coming at you has the unstoppable velocity of a truck with no brakes. You will find that you can tune in to subtle undercurrents that tell you so much more than the surface presentation. And you will be able to call out of hiding the true gifts and qualities of the other.

THE
Call

Even if you are feeling overstressed from dealing with negative energy that's like so many blood-sucking mosquitoes in a swamp, remind yourself that all energy comes at you in one form or another. You can master that energy, but that does not mean eliminating it or not opening yourself to experience it fully. Mastery means moving with it and transforming it. The world will always be this way. It is inherently unpredictable, and no fortress will protect you against it. And really, you don't want to live in such a fortress, for such places only bury your life force.

Remember the words of the Greek philosopher who said, "All things change." You must learn to dance with change. Allow yourself to surf the cresting wave of change. But learn to discern real change so that you are not caught in each succeeding bubble of fashion.

Study energy blockage and energy flow. Watch how energy expands and contracts. Become a witness of its ebb and flow as skillfully as a bird that knows the subtle shifts in tides and breezes or as any animal that reads the signals of approaching weather.

Become an energy connoisseur!

Don't get caught in the distorted mirror the bully creates to intimidate or control you. The bully's victory is to inhabit your inner voice, to shape-shift into your mind and emotions. Call up your power, not as a reflection of the same power that has dominated you, simply doubled in strength, but as the power of your own inherent vitality. Your own qualities are your true gold. The Sufis have a saying, "The real treasure is always buried under your feet." Dispel the voices that tell you that you have no treasure, that you are inferior in some way, that what you have to offer is insignificant. Those voices are the hidden voice of bullies. Bullies can be clever at transferring their own voices of inadequacy into their victims' beliefs about themselves.

Wake up every day and say, "I am a new creation!"

It is a great mystery, but the truth is, you are called to search for your essence and draw from it as your life source. We endure much testing, arising out of our own and others' false projections, until we find that original well of clear being within us. Mystics will tell you that your essence can never be touched or spoiled, but it *can* get covered over. If you find that is the case, belief is the deep antidote to confusion. Belief is the current that turns on the energy of transformation.

It may sound hackneyed to say, "Believe in yourself." The reason this can fail to reassure us is that we tend to believe in results rather than root causes. We want to channel energy into the places where we imagine things will be perfect. But that only leads us to become the banker, not the one who experiences real wealth. We miss the mark because we fail to trust the source. Rather than being a congealed energy or static reference point, belief is a dynamic place of trust and connection.

So let your belief flow. Let your belief shape the deepest trust, so that when you cooperate with the energy of the universe, it will guide you to be in alignment with your true nature.

All violence comes from falling out of alignment with yourself. You cannot force others to bring you back into alignment or have them become surrogates for your real needs.

Your soul, as a unique representative of the whole, calls you to remember who it is you really are. For it knows what no scientist can deny: all originates from a common source. Everything is itself and has its own nature but is also a part of the whole. If you can experience the fullness of that reality, you will know the peace that passes all understanding. And not only will you release any energy that keeps you from experiencing that peace but also you will be a wellspring of subtle and peaceful energy for others.

Reflection AND Practice

Everyone reading this book must deal with what Daniel Goleman calls "the chronic distractibility that has become the norm in modern life." As I noted earlier, so much has been written on contemplative and mindfulness practices that I think going over them here would be redundant. But it is worth underscoring that the mastery of energy must include the mastery of mental energy. Michael Singer's *The Untethered Soul: The Journey Beyond Yourself* gives the most clear and comprehensive description of how to master the "monkey mind."[6] Singer, whose own life is an example of masterful energetic flow, shows us the entanglement of mind and energy even at the subtlest levels. In several ways, this chapter has been influenced by one of his central ideas: that we must become deeply aware of the constant interactive relationship of consciousness and energy.

A consciousness dominated by fear or desire will attempt to push away or draw in those energies—or get hooked by its interactions with them. We have to sit further back in consciousness so we can allow the energy to move freely from a place of deep witnessing. The first way to cultivate that witness is by observing the ceaseless voice in your own head. Singer refers to that voice as "your roommate." As it turns out, your roommate has a lot of opinions, takes up a lot of space, and uses up a lot more of your energy than you realize.

I also recommend the work of B. Alan Wallace, who has given a lifetime to rigorous meditative practice and has participated in ongoing conversations between Buddhists and scientists. Of particular relevance to the theme of this chapter is his book *The Attention Revolution: Unlocking the Power of the Focused Mind*.[7] Wallace shares specific developmental practices, as well as deeper theoretical background. He understands the damage done by failing to master our attention:

Like a wild elephant, the untamed mind can inflict enormous damage on ourselves and those around us. In addition to oscillating between an attention deficit (when we are passive) and hyperactivity (when we are active), the normal, untrained mind constantly disgorges a toxic stream of wandering thoughts, then latches on to them obsessively, carried away by one story after another.

I recommend that however you do it, you meet your roommate. Take enough time to see how much violence he or she is doing to your psyche and what you might do once you track down this "person" in your house. You may be surprised at how sloppy, judgmental, anxious, and erratic this busy inhabitant is.

I truly believe that you should not feel intimidated by the claims of any approach to finding peace of mind. Maybe group chanting, *dhikr*, yoga, movement, varieties of breath work, or other approaches work better for you than "sitting." Find a practice that brings your energy into balance.

We have outlined some approaches to dealing with bullies. Please review the aikido approach recommended for each form of bullying. The important underlying mastery is to create an intention to care for the bully. This is essential. You cannot dissolve animosity with animosity. You cannot transform one energetic frequency with an identical frequency—they will simply combine to amplify that frequency. You cannot use the energy that has conditioned certain behaviors to change those behaviors. You have to come from love to transform anger; anger attempting to transform anger is called a shouting match. Recognize that bullying comes from a wound and, as a peacemaker, explore how you can help heal that wound even as you make sure that neither you nor others are hurt by it.

Remember that bullying extends from the crudest use of power to the subtlest of manipulations. Look around your home, your workplace, your society, and the world, and score on a scale of one to ten the bullying in each of these arenas and for each of the three categories of bullying we looked at (physical, emotional, and intellectual). The point of this exercise is twofold: First, it will help you identify the different kinds of bullying and where they show up in your life and the world around you. Second, it will train you to decipher these gradations of bullying we have been looking at, from the gross to the subtle.

As you identify the different kinds and different intensities of bullying on your chart, then ask yourself, "How do I experience and express compassion for these various kinds of bullies? How can I deal with them so they do not hurt me, others, or themselves?" The assignment can give you an idea of just how demanding this kind of peace work really is. You are asked to become a master in dissolving the harsh energy of blame, shame, and polarizing judgment. You are asked to gain insight into where your own energy is coming from and how, or whether, it is qualitatively different from those other harmful energies.

People get confused here because our conditioning tells us that harshness must be met with harshness, force met with greater force. You can get slammed for being *soft* on abusers or being *weak* in the face of evil. But what you are asked to do as an ambassador of peace is to be skillful at reading energy in ways that enable you to avoid harm and address root causes.

I remember I was once interviewed on NPR about the American intervention in Yugoslavia. I tried to orient my responses to a primary message: it is a little late to come to the human rights community, which documents the patterns of abuse that will inevitably erupt in major conflict, when that explosion has already happened. Let's do something about evil when we can do so peacefully and creatively. When the elements have combined to create H_2SO_4, the acid has been created. When brutal violence is boiling over, especially when massacres of civilians and genocidal acts are taking place, we are beyond prevention. In fact, we are morally required to intervene to save lives.

I have seen a fair amount of hand-wringing hypocrisy among peace activists who condemn any use of military force, when it is clear that if a murderer was in the act of mutilating their child, they would have no problem using violence to stop him. The consequence of ignoring any signal is that you will suffer greater consequences as a result. The old concept of the peace movement was that it started to organize when the drums of war were beginning to beat loud and clear. The emerging peace movement looks at the drum and says: This is how you use it to signal peace and pulse the heartbeat of connection. This is how you use the drum to signal dialogue and negotiation.

To what have you tuned your attention? Where is your energy being channeled—learning the intricate rhythms of the peace drum or drifting off until your ear cocks at the sound of the war drum? For once the drums of war have been sounded, our work is very different: we need to act strategically to stop the elements interacting instead of using our energy to remind people how deeply sulfuric acid burns away flesh.

Step back and ask yourself, Where am I putting my precious energy?

We also described the different ways people respond to difficult energy. These patterns often begin early in life. When dealing with difficult encounters with others, did you have a tendency to absorb it all and feel sorry for yourself? Or did you dismiss and even deny what happened by going into a fantasy world? Or were you able to hold your own while always trying to see the best in others? Choose four larger conflict situations that have occurred in your life, and review how you handled each of them.

Mastery comes with practice, and practice comes from encounter, not from theories. Your assignment, should you accept it, is to meet those energies you are always trying to avoid. When you learn how to dissolve their power over you and even dance with them, you will be well on your way to becoming a truly great ambassador, representing that great realm we have come to call peace.

Chapter 8

~

Achieving Peace through Creativity and Dialogue

When you familiarize yourself with the creativity now present in today's peace movement, it can inspire you tremendously—but it can also leave you feeling dismayed that so much great work is underreported. There are peace initiatives representing health professionals, media specialists, schoolchildren, city councils, clowns, academics, politicians, journalists, businesspeople, artists, and regular citizens putting their lives on the line to protect others.

In my own work, dialogue has been a key expression of my creativity. I have been privileged to facilitate and participate in a wide range of sustained dialogic contexts that have truly challenged me to be creative in ways I would not have imagined. Over the past twenty years, I have conducted and participated in

- dialogue exploring compassion and social healing with human rights and peace activists and those exposed to torture, violence, and occupation;

- dialogue on a mutual acknowledgment of wounding with Israelis, Palestinians, and international psychiatrists, psychologists, and social workers;
- dialogue on diverse topics of healing and peace with scientists and academics;
- dialogue focusing on collaboration rather than competition with consortia of nonprofit organizations;
- dialogue exploring the inner and outer aspects of activism with intergenerational social and sacred activists;
- dialogue on science, cosmology, and culture with physicists, thought leaders, and Native American elders;
- dialogue on cultural renewal with Irish and Icelandic social entrepreneurs and change agents; and
- dialogue with theorists and cultural leaders exploring integral evolution.

From that list, you can tell that I believe dialogue to be a central dimension of creative peacebuilding and nurturing a culture of peace. So, while the greater emphasis in this chapter is on dialogue because that is where I have had my own most formative experience, I want to affirm that dialogue is but one of a great many expressions of creativity in the field of peace work.

Let me begin with a story of one man's brilliant expression of creative dialogue when faced with a very threatening situation. One morning I was having breakfast in my high-mountain Colorado home listening to the radio when my attention was arrested. A person of no special notoriety and not a professional peacemaker was describing a riveting incident in which he was involved.

Julio Diaz was getting off a subway train in the Bronx intending to visit his favorite diner for a late-night meal when he was accosted. A teenager came up to him brandishing a knife and demanding that Julio hand over his wallet. Without hesitation Julio gave the youth his wallet, and the young man started to bolt toward the stairs when Julio called after him. He asked his youthful assailant if he also needed his coat, as it was a cold night. The youth came to a halt, flabbergasted.

Julio told him that he thought that if he was so desperate to steal this small amount of money, maybe he also needed a coat to keep warm. He also said that he would be happy to invite the young man to have dinner with him at his favorite diner, because he looked as if he could use a good meal and company. Hesitantly and suspiciously, the teenager agreed to have dinner with Julio.

When they got to the diner, Julio was greeted by people who knew him, and throughout the meal the waiter, the chef, and others came by to chitchat. The young man was amazed at how friendly people were and how much they loved Julio. When it came time to pay the bill, Julio indicated to the young man that he could not pay for obvious reasons, and the teenager responded by giving him back his wallet. Julio paid the bill and then offered to give the young man twenty dollars, which he obviously needed, but on one condition: that he trade in his knife for the money. Julio had disarmed his assailant with skill and great compassion.

Now that is how to make peace! Julio did not allow himself to be triggered. He kept himself centered in the other person's need. And he responded with courage and creativity to affirm his own deepest values of human solidarity. Perhaps there are a number of ways to protect oneself, disarm an assailant, and even give him a lesson in humanity, but this approach to centering one's energy and establishing dialogue deserves the attention of anyone called to be a creative peacemaker.

Visitors from another galaxy would probably say that what seems to be the defining difference between humans and other species is our creativity. Then they would note that this creativity is used to liberate people's highest qualities, as well as to unleash their basest instincts. They would see how imaginative we are at enhancing life and yet how ingenious we are at destroying it. Imagine with me that they quickly come to the conclusion that Earth will flourish if all of our creativity is directed at the former, and then they decide to check back in a few millennia to see if we have learned to shed those massively destructive instincts. As they head back to Planet Paradiso, they reflect, "Just a matter of time before they fully evolve!"

But is this only a fairy tale?

Are we really going to evolve into one big planetary peace circle? Are we really going to slough off greed and prejudice? Are we going to stop the exploitation and all the other ways we turn the energy of the universe into unskillful behavior or brute force? Well, the answer is a qualified yes. Yes, we are evolving, and our destiny is to evolve beyond ego fixations and attachments. But I doubt very much if we will witness everyone on earth sitting in a huge circle singing kumbaya, because in a dynamic universe there will always be different songs, different ways of communing, and profoundly different ways of expressing community and solidarity. The one thing we can all agree upon is that this is not a static universe but rather a dynamic, evolving, and interdependent system, which also goes for all of our social systems. Understanding the nature of its dynamism is essential for advanced and creative peace work. In a world of ceaseless change and infinite variables, creativity becomes the key to expressing meaning in ways that optimize diversity and sustain coherence.

Evolving systems have rhythms and cycles. Part of nature's dynamic design is that contraction and loss are an integral part of expansion and recovery. One theory, subscribed to by leading historians and social theorists, says that history itself reveals cyclical patterns in human development, even as the entire process slowly moves forward. Cycles seem to go through four stages: the beginning of a new era follows a period of crisis or catastrophe; this leads to an era of prosperity and cultural flowering that sees the maturation and expression of new forms; in the third stage, a peak has been reached, and cracks begin to appear in existing structures; and finally, the old order collapses, crisis shatters anything that is not enduring, and the next cycle begins.

From the birth and expansion of the universe to the whirling activity inside every atom in existence, the cosmos is characterized by a perpetual *dynamic and evolutionary* process. That is a nonnegotiable part of the design. Peace is unimaginable if we freeze the creative quest to know and understand the very nature of the universe and our role in it and instead declare that we have arrived at a final truth. Any such declarations become a source of conflict because they take a part of the truth and project it as the whole. Can you see that every time we go into paroxysms of violent conflict, it is because the dynamic truths of an evolving universe have been frozen around a prescribed way of behaving, thinking, or being? Yet in the twenty-first century people are still killed because they cross the line from one such allegiance to another.

Numerous forces seek to stomp on human creativity. But it is only through the unfettered interplay of creativity in service to the cause of life that peace becomes possible. Peace penetrates the armature of false certainty and dissolves all claims of exclusive rights to the truth. To accomplish this, peace work must be highly creative and even spontaneous, as it was with Julio Diaz.

It fills me with awe to witness and participate in creative actions to liberate people and to give voice to the voiceless. What captivated me to work for Amnesty International was the desire to free the prisoner, to enter a story where a person's freedom of expression had been cut off and to use whatever creative means we could to change that story. The lonely and deprived Constantino Coronet, who was a prisoner of conscience in Paraguay, received a crumpled note thrown into his cell. Listen to his response to this simple act by one person to creatively reach out by writing a letter to a prisoner far away:

> For years, I was held in a tiny cell. My only human contact was with my torturers. For two and a half of those years, I did not experience the glance of a human face, see a green leaf. My only company was the cockroaches and mice. The only daylight that entered my cell was through a small opening at the top of one wall. For eight months, I had my hands and feet tied. On Christmas Eve, the door to my cell opened, and the guard tossed in a crumpled piece of paper. I moved as best I could to pick up the paper. It said simply, "Constantino, do not be discouraged; we know you are alive." It was signed "Monica" and had the Amnesty International candle on it. Those words saved my life and my sanity. Eight months later I was set free.

Creativity and dialogue

As mentioned above, my own experience of peak creativity in peace-making has been through a variety of forms of dialogue that unblock people and free them to express heartfelt truths. I have seen how dialogue allows people to experience community, share the exploration of ideas, evolve new kinds of consensus where none existed before, and create fields of collective resonance.

In the last fifty years, the peace movement has been learning new approaches to dialogue that have several common characteristics: they integrate ancient circle practice, explore consensus, and catalyze deep conversation about vision and values. In addition, we have been learning how to integrate new discoveries in order to achieve a better match of the form of a dialogue with its intended function.

- *We have learned* how to hold "deep space" so that emotionally charged experiences can be shared in safe and psychologically nuanced environments.
- *We have learned* how to tap into fields of collective intelligence and group wisdom, and in doing so, we have discovered how to build nonhierarchical learning communities and to move into intersubjective learning environments.
- *We have learned* how to listen with both heart and mind and to suspend polarizing judgment before it severs deep communication.
- *We have learned* that we can be brilliant when the busy mind is still and deeply receptive.
- *We have learned* that "open space" and other self-organizing processes can allow us to hear new voices, gather a greater range of perspectives, and explore topics of genuine interest that lead to decentralized agenda setting.

Many formats exist for applying these discoveries, and peacebuilders are constantly creating new formats and creatively redesigning existing ones. Existing formats include a variety of circle processes, town hall meetings, small- and large-group interactive processes, conversation cafés, panels, debates, lectures, and creative online applications of the above.

In my long work in this field, I have come to the conclusion that communication for peace has seven major functions: presentation, council, inquiry, conversation, deep dialogue, mediation, and the exploration of consensus. No matter how creative we get in our formats, the deepest creativity occurs when form serves function. This means that the processes we apply must be able to deliver the accomplishment of key functions.

Presentation

Good presentation is simply about making sure that certain concepts and information are made clear, that they are understood to the extent possible, and that there are opportunities to question, appreciate, or challenge as necessary. Presentational skills and technologies are experiencing an explosion of creativity. This is exciting because it allows for the widespread dissemination, analysis, and discussion of new ideas and pivotal information. The emerging peace movement is able to present the depth and complexity of a culture of peace through a wide range of presentational modalities, from brilliant advocacy campaigns and public demonstrations to art, music, movie, and video. Not only do we have interactive Internet networking and conferencing to mobilize and inform people, but we also have extraordinary teleconferencing capacities. For example, the Shift Network organizes an annual Peace Week global telesummit, bringing together more than thirty thousand people from forty countries to listen to the world's leading peacebuilders, ask them questions, comment on their presentations, and share concerns. This is just one example of how peacebuilding is getting very creative! Never have the opportunities been greater to get our message across in ways that inform, inspire, and activate people.

Council

The essence of being in council is that people are invited to speak what is on their mind without debate or immediate discussion. Space is created for people to absorb contrasting opinions and perspectives so that those who are speaking know they are not going to be pounced on.

Believe it or not, one of the hardest things to do is to get people to speak the truth. Creating the conditions for truth telling sometimes requires our best creativity. It can be particularly difficult in group settings: people are afraid they'll upset the apple cart or that others will turn on them if they say what is on their mind. But as I have noted repeatedly in this book, if people do not share their truth, peace will be subverted in insidious ways. However the sharing of personal truth may be carried out, the job of the peace ambassador is to call it out and ask the group to practice some form of council in an attempt to get people to give voice to their truth. This can involve creatively stepping up and pointing to the denial when a group is not facing the fact that the unspoken is really the driver of agendas.

The peacebuilder must make clear that the emphasis is on deep listening and the honoring of honesty. And the council must agree that the process will not be rushed or deprioritized. When people recognize that truth is the biggest agenda, seemingly more urgent agendas tend to fall into place.

Inquiry

The truth can appear to be very solid—the core problem I identified earlier—but a little probing usually reveals that every truth has boundaries of connection with other truths, and that all truth depends on an agreement about very basic facts. As we note in the next chapter on systems thinking, truth is more relative than fixed. To establish a valid truth, people must first explore it in order to understand its context and its connection to a greater whole. In the pursuit of social or cultural truth, we have seen a blossoming of inquiry processes in recent years, as people give themselves space to move beyond the classical scientific method.

Inquiry does not presuppose agreement or disagreement. Good inquiry process recognizes that presuming agreement can be a way of silencing dissent and overlooking nuances, which become so rich when explored.

Inquiry requires an overall commitment to ask questions, explore their implications, test their reality, and then see what they might look like when applied, after which one may evaluate the results and do further reflection to see what is next. Look around you at the institutions that make a commitment to inquiry process, and you will see they are the healthiest and most creative.

A number of specific inquiry processes can be used to explore a question facing a group and to resolve how to move forward. One that I particularly like is called *appreciative inquiry*. This approach occurs in four phases:

1. *discovery*—focusing on appreciating what is best about what is
2. *dreaming*—allowing for an unfettered exploration of what could be
3. *designing*—determining what should be
4. *delivering*—deciding what will be

Conversation

Conversation is about hearing all the voices and letting meaning be woven out of their interactions rather than forced upon people by someone's agenda. Conversation is ideal for exploring values. Innovations in orchestrating large-scale conversations have allowed us to cultivate collective intelligence more than ever. One example of a creative conversational approach is known as the World Café, a process that was developed by Juanita Brown and David Isaacs, of Mill Valley, California.[1] According to Otto Scharmer, a senior lecturer at the MIT Sloan School of Management and the author of *Theory U: Learning from the Future as It Emerges*, "What is missing in the crisis of our current age is a social technology to access the collective wisdom of diverse and distributed communities. The World Café is an innovative social technology that embodies the principles and practices of a new type of collective conversation that can access this wisdom." The key organizing principles of the World Café are worth noting. The café aims to

- set a clear context for the topic to be explored
- create a hospitable space to allow people to participate in conversation
- explore questions that really matter to the participants
- encourage contributions from everyone
- connect diverse perspectives
- listen together for patterns and insights
- share collective discoveries

Also worthy of note is the Conversation Café movement started by Vicki Robin, Susan Partnow, and Habib Rose in Seattle. This approach to stirring meaningful conversations in coffee shops and cafés has now become an international movement. Peace is about talking to one another, and now the conversation can be global.

As Margaret Wheatley says in her book *Turning to One Another: Simple Conversations to Restore Hope to the Future*: "Conversation, however, takes time. We need time to sit together, to listen, to worry and dream together. As this age of turmoil tears us apart, we need to reclaim time to be together. Otherwise, we cannot stop the fragmentation."

Deep dialogue

Since 1998, Leroy Little Bear, a Blackfoot elder and sage, has presided over the Language of Spirit dialogues between leading physicists, scientists, and thought leaders on the one hand and Native and indigenous leaders and wisdom keepers on the other.[2] He begins each dialogue by reminding people to suspend their "tacit infrastructures." True dialogue cannot occur if we are narrating internally what others say through the prism of our own opinions, beliefs, and worldview. Then we are really not listening to them; we are listening to our own view of them and their ideas. Our tacit infrastructures are those unspoken assumptions we make about everything and everyone around us. They hold us inside the solidity of what we think we know. But deep dialogue asks us to let go and to explore the unknown without a lot of internal commentary, which diminishes our ability to be present for others. As poet Samuel Taylor Coleridge reminded us, no work of art can be truly appreciated until we "suspend disbelief." Dialogue is similar; it invites us to enter fresh territory, where we can know the world differently and see with new eyes. In this sense, deep dialogue is a creative form that allows for exploration of *the ground of being, the boundaries of knowledge, and the revelatory power of human experience and story*. It can also open up a depth field where awareness can creatively stimulate *new insight.*

I truly believe that the most sacred and beloved community can be created through deep dialogue. When people truly sense they are not going to be judged and when they can feel an openness to what they have to say, the quality and creativity of their interaction with the group are greatly enhanced. In working to create such safe contexts in my own work, I have witnessed a former Nazi and the daughter of Holocaust survivors commune together in dialogue. I have witnessed former militants embrace each other's humanity, who in a different time would have carried murderous enmity. I have seen victims open up the depth of their wounding to representatives of their perpetrators. I have seen survivors of genocide uplift others with their capacity to move beyond unspeakable brutality. In my own experience, there is nothing more humanizing than to participate in dialogue such as this, where people go to the heart of human suffering and explore how to transform a world that inflicts so much pain.

There is no single form of deep dialogue, but it is essential that deep listening be present and that concentrated awareness build in the group field. People experience an intensity of hearts and minds connecting in an amplified container that opens up depth perception and insight. Some refer to this as an experience of a presence that transcends but includes individual presence.

Of special note is a process known as Bohmian dialogue, named after physicist David Bohm. Bohm felt that "a thoroughgoing suspension of tacit individual and cultural infrastructures, in the context of full attention to their contents, frees the mind to move in new ways. . . . The mind is then able to respond to *creative new perceptions* going beyond the particular points of view that have been suspended."[3] He saw dialogue as harvesting a field of collective intelligence. In this form of dialogue, you listen so attentively that you do not rehearse in your mind what you are going to say if you are the next to speak. With your mind saturated in attention to the other and to the group context, what you will say will be much more alive and spontaneous.

Mediation

Johan Galtung is one of the fathers of contemporary peace and conflict-resolution studies.[4] In 1995, he helped mediate differences between Ecuador and Peru, which had fought three wars over an uninhabited region. As a result of Galtung's creative mediation, the warring countries made peace and created a bi-national eco-reserve.

Galtung grappled with the fact that most approaches to mediation lacked creativity and ended with winners and losers or with a compromise that made no one happy. Instead, the solution should represent a win-win and give all parties an opportunity to offer their best. Behavioral scientists have pointed out that people will cheat and even damage their own interests when they suspect that they will be exploited in some way. We behave badly when trust breaks down. But if trust is established, we are often more collaborative and even generous. Galtung makes the distinction between "negative peace" and "positive peace": the latter requires trust, collaboration, and engagement, whereas the former creates accommodations based on fear and distrust. Now the hunt is on to structure mediation so that it brings out the best in people.

More practitioners have begun to explore what is called transformative mediation. J. Kim Wright speaks to this in *Lawyers as Peacemakers: Practicing Holistic, Problem-Solving Law*:

The focus of transformative mediation is not only on resolution but provides conscious emphasis on transforming interactions from negative and destructive to positive and constructive. Practitioners use the complementary models of empowerment and recognition. The transformative framework for mediation seeks to help people regain their footing and shift back to a restored sense of strength or confidence in self—the empowerment shift—and openness or responsiveness to the other—the recognition shift. The transformation of the relationship dynamic is seen as more important than the presenting conflict.[5]

As Marshall Rosenberg points out in his system of nonviolent communication, the source of a dispute isn't really the problem that is presented; the source is the rupture in the world of relationship. The only way to deal with that rupture is to recognize the mutuality of unmet needs and try to meet them.

Negotiation is a step up from mediation but has many of its elements. High-level peace negotiations are the work of professionals, although William Ury has done a great deal to make that work more accessible. Ury is the author of *Getting to Yes: Negotiating Agreement without Giving In*. He is also a cofounder of the Harvard Program on Negotiation. He emphasizes the role of "the third force," or surrounding community, which can play an important role in nurturing dialogue among the conflicted parties.[6]

The exploration of consensus

Democracy has been reduced to a competition for majority rule. Success is seen as polarizing the citizenry to gain sufficient votes to win an advantage over opponents. Collaborative politics is almost anathema these days in the United States. The notion that democracy is fulfilled by striving for consensus is ignored by vested interests that feed off feverish competition. At the end of the day, the polarity is never as real as it is presented or manufactured to be. And we advance every time we forge a genuine consensus.

The Latin root of the word *consensus* means to "feel together." Consensus is about giving consent yet not necessarily agreeing with every detail of a proposed course of action. It is about creating solidarity with others to improve the life and health of the whole. Consensus is about supporting inclusion without diluting principles to the degree that they are rendered meaningless.

Consensus process is iterative—that is, it goes back over different viewpoints to sift threads of connection and points of significant departure. Consensus allows itself to be informed by dissent. It keeps homing in on the benefits of proceeding on a certain course while evaluating the disadvantages and bearing in mind the disagreements.

The Occupy movement has created renewed interest in consensus decision-making processes. While it is easier and quicker to have an up-or-down vote, the Occupy participants clearly demonstrate that consensus process creates a much deeper synthesis of a group's diverse ideas and ensures a much greater degree of collective buy-in.

Consensus process is evolutionary, a reflection of our evolving creativity. Consensus has the following features:

- It calls for optimal collaboration rather than maximum competition.
- It strives to be egalitarian rather than controlled by special interests.
- It invites the full inclusion of all stakeholders rather than the selective exclusion of some.
- It challenges everyone to engage and participate rather than succumb to passivity.

The renaissance of creativity for peace

Not a day goes by that we cannot be truly in awe at the ingenuity and creativity of human beings to make peace a reality. Severe as our challenges are, and devastatingly cruel, cynical, and indifferent as we can be as a species, from where I sit, the world cannot but rise out of the ashes of its disastrous lack of skillfulness. There is simply too much creativity afoot. So many are now involved in the mirroring of compassion, courage, and passion to transform our world that it may only be a matter of time before we reach a critical mass of peacebuilders.

In my view, one person who is paradigmatic of this creativity is Nipun Mehta. In his early twenties, Nipun Mehta was on his way to becoming a successful Silicon Valley computer geek. He could have had it all—recognition, wealth, and a California dream home. But for him that was not a call to creativity but rather an invitation to live a conformist and conventional lifestyle. Something was calling him to live the true adventure of evolving and of living at the very edge of his capacities.

One day he and a few friends went to a homeless shelter as volunteers. Not long after, Nipun listened to a dramatic inner call to simply give his life to service. In doing so, he had to surrender any idea of organizing his life around money and success the way most people do. Some looked at him as an individual who was dropping out, but he was really dropping in. He was dropping in to a state of spiritual surrender.

He started to organize volunteers—a lot of techie volunteers—to help nonprofits that needed support, and he created an organization now called ServiceSpace. At the same time, he convened friends and those directly involved in his service projects to meet regularly for spiritual talks and meditation. From the outset, Nipun connected inner practice and outer service. Relentlessly, he pushed the boundary of the concept that it is in giving that we receive.

I first connected with him when I was executive director of the Seva Foundation. The foundation, named after the Sanskrit word for service, was founded by contemporary guru Ram Dass (a.k.a. Harvard professor Richard Alpert), clown extraordinaire Wavy Gravy (a.k.a. Hugh Romney), and doctor-cum-entrepreneur Larry Brilliant. This seemingly out-there crew have created a very effective organization combating blindness and promoting community development. I invited Nipun to join the board after seeing an article about him playfully titled "Nipun Mehta—the Guru of Silicon Valley." Every interaction I have had with him since then has confirmed that he holds an inner core of peace and stillness as he engages passionately and creatively with the world.

Today ServiceSpace has 350,000 subscribers and has donated in volunteer time the equivalent of tens of millions of dollars. Most of the projects it has incubated are based in the concept of "gift economy" that Nipun has been developing over the years. From Karma Kitchen restaurants in different cities to pay-it-forward rickshaws in India, Nipun and his organization show us how to give and how to creatively make peace. They show us how to integrate spirituality and action. They teach how peace work can be high tech and high touch. They remind us that the path of service is the path to peace.[7]

One small organization is actually called Creativity for Peace. Here is yet another microcosm of what is possible in creative peace work. Based out of Santa Fe, New Mexico, it brings together Israeli and Palestinian teenage girls for a camp experience where they dialogue, converse, create art, dance, and learn to communicate what is really in their hearts. The program is hugely healing for the participants. It is a reminder that small initiatives can deeply transform lives. Now visualize tens of thousands of small- to medium-sized peace initiatives blossoming across the planet, and you begin to see the first flowering of a global renaissance of peace and creativity.

The River Phoenix Center for Peacebuilding in Gainesville, Florida, has a simple slogan: "It is time we make peacebuilding a co-ordinated community effort." The founders of this highly innovative center see it as a potential model to be used in cities across the world. Founded only recently, the center is already creating partnerships with law enforcement, schools and academic institutions, businesses, and neighborhood groups. A central motif of their work is that we can heal division in communities, apply restorative justice approaches much more widely, and acquire the basic tools of peacebuilding. Imagine a center like this in your town or city—then set about creating one![8]

Here's a final example: Maybe you will have seen at some point one of those peace poles with the words "May Peace Prevail on Earth" written in different languages. Japanese spiritual teacher Masahisa Goi had a creative vision of world peace and began the initiative in 1955.

Today more than two hundred thousand poles have been placed in two hundred countries around the world. They carry inside them scrolls written with deep love and intention at a beautiful and serene sanctuary under Mount Fuji. In 2006, I joined ten thousand people at this site, where representatives of the world's religious traditions prayed together for peace. Circled by the flag of every nation on earth, I felt that Master Goi's vision of world peace would one day be fulfilled.

As Rumi said, "There are a thousand ways to kneel and kiss the ground." And there are limitless ways to practice peace. Now let yourself be inspired to get creative!

THE Call

Trust in your own creativity. This is essential. It is good to be appreciative of other people's creativity but not when it inhibits your own. We can find ourselves worshipping the brilliance of others and putting them on a pedestal in ways that shrink our own sense of capacity.

You don't have to be like those you admire. You are called to be true to yourself. Start with gratitude, which has the power to transform the seed of envy into self-empowerment. Be grateful for who you are and admit that you are a creative being.

Sometimes when we are blocked and feel a wall of resistance to being creative in expressing ourselves, the blockage is like a cork in a vat. We experience the blockage as being generalized, but it is in fact usually quite specific. Feeling that you will be blamed or ridiculed if things go wrong, feeling that you will lose control, feeling that you have no right to lead, feeling that you have no idea what you are doing, feeling that you will be on your own—all these and more can be blockages to creative action. Find the voice—that specific voice—which is holding you back and say to it, "You do not have the power to kill my creativity. I am a creative being." And whether it is stepping onto a podium, walking into a classroom, posting a video clip on YouTube, unfurling a campaign plan, starting an organization, leaving home to go where you feel you are needed most, starting a dialogue with those you are in disagreement with, or simply reinventing and healing your relationship to anything or anyone who has stood in your path—tell yourself that you have made a commitment to liberate your own being. In fact, you are going to get out of the way and let the larger energy of evolutionary change come through you.

I agree with those who say not to take everything so personally. Think of yourself as a conduit for energy that wants to shake up the whole botched-up status quo. Think of energy as collective property owned by all, to be used on behalf of all. Now see that energy not as dangerous but as consciousness eager to serve the emancipation of all. Pure energy is humility and has no ego. So step into it and surrender to its grace and power.

You don't need to underestimate the forces that want to block you—they are great. They have armies killing civilians, they have terrorists wanting to take you back to the Stone Age, they have corporate agents of every kind of exploitation and repression, they have legions of seduction and distraction. But these forces are the fiercely negative entropy of dying worlds. Stare too long into their eyes, and they will pull you into their catastrophic end games. Spend your time in defiance of them, and you will be spun in the inescapable vortex of their polarities. So by all means, tell yourself the stakes are very high, for they are. But once you know how high they are, you will feel the surging energy of the future calling you anyway, and when you step aside and let it speak through you and be you—you will create! And what you create will be peace.

Reflection AND Practice

How are you experiencing this renaissance of creativity, when the so-called average person is able to engage and have an impact as never before? Creativity is not about being superbusy; it is about high-quality interventions. Think of the range of expressions of your creativity, which go from being quietly effective to boldly and publicly declared.

Review each of the seven functions of communication for peace, and explore your current level of creativity. How can you be more creative, or as I like to frame it, How can you express your innate creativity?

It all begins with presentation. This is where you need to get something across that is going to make a difference, something that is going to lead to greater peace. Maybe you need to present the idea that deeper dialogue is needed in your home or office or place of worship. How are you going to present in a way that you will be heard? How can you avoid triggering a rejection response?

People can spend a lot of time organizing and planning peace-related activities and then put "marketing" last—as if "How do we creatively communicate all this?" is an afterthought. In reality, "How am I presenting myself and my ideas?" is a fundamental question for a peace ambassador. "How am I going to present to others the need for dialogue, conversation, mediation, or consensus building?" Spend time with these questions, and do not allow your enthusiasm to trip you up because you got so passionate and excited that you forgot to think about how your ideas might be received. The missionary's zealotry rarely works; putting yourself in the shoes of the other does.

Ask yourself next, "Who is it that I really need to engage with in conversation or dialogue to bring about more peace?" You may be surprised to find that you don't need to go as far as you thought. Try your neighbor. It is always easier to promote a peaceful cause than to engage in peace making. It is important to support peace in places like Afghanistan and Darfur, but because the scale of bigotry or antagonism at home is not as great, hardly means that it should be ignored. We have to taste peace, not just advocate peace.

In Iceland after the financial collapse, people felt betrayed but also recognized that they themselves had participated in the whole illusory materialist bubble, as I pointed out in chapter 3. They recognized they had lost their way. Bjarni S. Jonsson, a student of Spiral Dynamics guru Don Beck, helped organize public conversations in Iceland for more than twenty thousand people. The conversations focused on exploring and sharing core values. Now you may not need to invite tens of thousands of people to a values conversation, but how about twenty in a World Café? (For more information on the World Café, check out its website.)

God gave Moses tablets of stone to communicate his commandments, but we have been given the Internet to communicate in any language at hyperspeeds, linking bodies of research, data, and images. This technology is not going away: the computers we use to text and chat are a thousand times more advanced than those that got men to the moon, and the ones that are coming are ten thousand times more advanced than those we are currently using. When Deepak Chopra tweets, he reaches about a million people. Every peace meme that reaches and expands people's consciousness will help permeate the collective field. Don't think you're just another drop in the bucket; instead, think how a billion drops change the tide.

Creativity and courage go hand in hand. The Theater of Witness performance that I observed in Northern Ireland, where real members of the community from all sides of the "divide" told their stories to the public, took passion and guts. Each person needed to go through an intense preparatory process to be able to stand on a public stage and not only tell his or her story but also tell it in the company of those who had been perpetrators and antagonists.

Only you can know where you need to cross the threshold of fear, self-doubt, or the intimidation of others to live your courage. Truly the greatest creativity emerges when people cross that threshold. Sometimes we are called on to face down tyranny, and sometimes it even takes courage to soften our hearts and smile. It takes courage to make peace.

Chapter 9

~

Peace Work and Whole-Systems Shift

You may remember that strange song "Dry Bones": "Dem bones, dem bones, dem dry bones. Now hear the word of the Lord. Toe bone's connected to the foot bone. Foot bone's connected to the ankle bone. . . . " And on it goes, connecting the skeletal parts of the human body, all the while exhorting us to "hear the word of the Lord."

This folksy song reminds us that we are always in a discovery process about the relationship between the parts and the whole. As it suggests, the more you see and connect the parts, the more you affirm their sacred relationship. And when you move beyond the image of the mechanical dancing skeleton to the reality of the overwhelming symphony of the human body, with its network of trillions of cells communicating and pulsing in an ever-shifting biochemical and electromagnetic field of energy—it is then that you feel awe.

The challenge, of course, is that this vast interplay of life is covered by a layer of skin. It comes in a package. Our attention gets fixated on the design of the package, does it not? We tend to put a lot of energy into making the package look good and fret when it doesn't. Then, when the contents of the package start to break down, we seek the best medical or pharmaceutical fix rather than look at the resources that reside in the gift of consciousness.

Luckily, some of the most creative scientific exploration has begun to reveal how consciousness itself is an integral dimension of the inner design. Mind-body interactions are not separate but profoundly interconnected in ways we are still trying to appreciate and understand better. As never before, we are beginning to map the world concealed inside the skin, all the way to the inscrutable origins of consciousness and the energetic substrate of matter itself, and then on to learning just how these two elements interact with each other as part of a whole system. But we have much to learn. Biologists still do not understand what animates life. They have gone to great lengths to understand the parts and their interactions, but the whole eludes them.

The same is true of the universe: we have truly amazing discoveries in physics, quantum physics, and astrophysics, but we still face superordinate questions about the nature of pervasive dark energy, how energy binds into matter, what banged the big bang, and how many universes might exist that may be parallel or bleed into one another. "The word of the Lord" is written in a language that we are a long way from fully deciphering.

As we celebrate all the progress made in legal systems and global governance, we also see that we have much work to do to optimize them. The impressive body of international law sets forth an inspiring vision of legal protections to be incorporated into national laws, but in reality implementation is mixed and enforcement subject to political considerations. Despite its considerable achievements, the United Nations is chronically politicized and bullied by the permanent members of the Security Council. Our progress in transforming oppressive societies into democratic systems of governance also represents a benchmark in human evolution, but democracy has proven vulnerable to manipulation by economic and other vested interests. Our systemic challenges appear to some as gaping inadequacies that must be exposed and dealt with, while these same challenges go unnoticed by others.

How we behave is influenced by what we see within the limits of what we know. What we perceive is influenced by what we know and what we believe and what we believe we know. In turn, collective perception and thus collective behavior are organized around a common agreement about knowledge and belief.

Because of our limited perceptions, we will always claim *the part* to be *the whole* until we know and believe otherwise. And as history shows us, we will repeatedly proclaim the part is the whole to protect structures we have created to reinforce that belief—even when new knowledge challenges it. In this sense, it is true that knowledge is power.

More often than not, crude power likes to sustain itself around the continuation of certain beliefs rather than support the acquisition of knowledge. That is why tyranny wants to suppress knowledge and new ideas and to enforce existing beliefs. And this is why eventually all tyranny falls, because gaining knowledge seems to be an emergent property of the human evolutionary process. We are designed as creatures to grow in knowledge, and whoever tries to inhibit that design may delay but will never arrest evolutionary progress.

While it may seem that this discussion has entered very complex territory, one thing stands out in clear relief: we will never have peace as long as we have attachment to the part rather than the whole. Peace does not grow out of being a partisan for the part. Peace work is about engaging in processes that reveal the larger story. It is about revealing the hidden design of our interdependence, so often masked by social and ideological facades that stand for mere partial interests. It is about standing up for the parts that are overlooked or suppressed. It is about telling "inconvenient truths" and challenging the many half-truths that keep us separate.

For many of us, cultivating peace is a journey of intense discovery as we begin to perceive the patterns of relatedness and connection we were previously blind to. Once we experience the potential for the social organism to function as a healthy, interdependent body, we begin to glimpse how the entire global body can some day function as one in a state of peace.

But we don't have to create a perfect society before we attempt to heal the world. Changes in the parts and changes in the whole go both ways. Healthy systems have intensely accurate feedback loops and are constantly adjusting as a result.

Mapping the whole

Arthur Koestler coined the term *holarchy* to help us see that nature and the greater cosmos of which we are a part are not structured as simple hierarchies defined by who or what is on top. The universe is instead organized around *holons*. A holon is something that is whole in itself but at the same time part of a greater whole. This gives us the image of a nested reality—for example, in the way that individuals are nested in families, and families are nested in communities, and so on.

Joachim Wolf, in his book *Understanding the Grand Design*, lists what he calls holonic principles. Here is one of those principles: *The whole and its parts are one, when viewed from the dimensional level of the whole.* This is a simple formulation, but so powerful. The representative of peace has to get a wide-angle vision to articulate the "dimensional" perspective of the greatest wholeness and inclusion. The great visionaries are always trying to move us to that higher ground where we can experience something greater than our allegiance to the parts.

Martin Luther King Jr. was one such visionary, always a voice for the rights of minorities in the context of the fulfillment of the rights and destiny of the whole. "Now is the time to make real the promises of democracy," he declared in his famous "I Have a Dream" speech. "Now is the time to rise from the dark and desolate valley of segregation to the sunlit path of racial justice. Now is the time to lift our nation from the quicksands of racial injustice to the solid rock of brotherhood. Now is the time to make justice a reality for all of God's children."

But Wolf points out a related principle: *The whole is invisible from the lower dimensional parts.* And still another: *The different aspects of the whole appear as separate parts when viewed from the lower dimensional level of the parts.* This would suggest another aspect of the peacemaker's work: since the parts cannot see the whole and everything looks separate to them, peace work must help the parts experience their connection to one another before they can perceive the whole.

These principles were beautifully reflected in the movie *Invictus*. The national rugby team was an image of the separations and divisions that existed under the Apartheid regime in South Africa. Mandela was in his first term as president of the first post-Apartheid government, and his task was to unite a torn country. The new government needed to show the country how it could win by joining forces. Mandela, prompted by Don Beck, an international systems theorist whose character does not appear in the movie, pushes to support a biracial national rugby team. The object was to unite the team members and to win the enthusiastic support of the whole nation to secure the 1995 Rugby World Cup. It was important that all the parts see how together they could unify to become invincible.

Similarly, Paul Kagame, who became president of Rwanda in 2000, had a grievous division to heal in a nation where the differences between Hutu and Tutsi had been cynically engineered by his predecessors. I visited Rwanda in 2008, fourteen years after the genocide. It was an intense experience for me, as I had done everything in my power as the director of the Washington office of Amnesty International to alert the United States and other governments of the gathering human rights crisis in Rwanda in the lead-up to those unspeakable crimes that the international community failed to prevent. More than two hundred thousand Tutsi are buried at the Genocide Memorial in Kigali. I also visited a church where ten thousand Tutsi, mostly women and children, were slaughtered. Yet fourteen years later, more than half the country identified themselves as Rwandan before any other identity. The level of healing was extraordinary, and the sense of emerging pride in their peaceful and orderly society was palpable. Whatever the shortcomings of Kagame and his government, they made reconciliation a priority and created a sense of national identity that people could be genuinely proud of. The parts could find in the new identity of a society freed of corruption and striving for equal opportunity what they could not experience as competing identities.

The great wheel of peace

One of the leaders in *mapping the whole* in peace work is Avon Mattison.[1] Avon has dedicated her life to promoting a systems approach to creating a culture of peace. Thirty years ago she was among the first to articulate clearly that a culture of peace can fully emerge only when we think holistically; to illustrate that principle she used what she called the *peace wheel*. The first spoke of the wheel consists of new forms of governance and a re-visioning of law and society to align justice with societal healing. Another spoke is the integration of science and technology into peace paradigms in contrast to their service to militarism, weapons, and corporate exploitation. Peace education, the education of the whole person, and the development of a conscious and mature media committed to telling the whole story constitute another spoke in the peace wheel. Other spokes include sustainable and ecologically sensitive economic paradigms; conscious business and fair trade; interfaith paradigms and inclusive spirituality; holistic health and healthy relationships at all levels of the social order; and the final spoke, the transformation of cultural values and social norms to support nonviolence and peace. All of these subsystems have to synchronize in some fundamental way for the wheel of peace to turn current planetary conditions into a healthy, just, sustainable, fulfilling, and peaceful global civilization.

It doesn't require rocket science to see that the spokes are going in all directions, often behaving like autonomous units oblivious to the health of the whole system. For example, the spoke standing for economics is not driven by a motivation to optimize health and well-being and is prone to pursue profit at the expense of environmental sustainability.

Profiteering is a huge virus—the equivalent of a killer pandemic. Since 1970, we have lost more than one-third of Earth's species and have poisoned land, sea, and air to a degree that defies every rational indicator of what is acceptable. We are the only species destroying its own habitat and seeding catastrophe for its own offspring. Schoolchildren, for good reason, increasingly express anxiety and fear about the environmental degradation of the planet.

In the absence of current human activity, our planet and its systems would self-correct quickly. What nature does well is represent the whole, promoting the interdependence of all life. Nature's job is to serve life abundant, and we interfere with this job at our peril. As Kenny Ausubel, the inspired cofounder of Bioneers, warns us: "Nature will never support the destruction of all life forms in favor of one species." In fact, it supports abundant biodiversity with principles such as kinship, symbiosis, and community. When nature mirrors for us a sustainable life, why do we choose greed, leading to our own demise?

Peacebuilders must take on whole-system wreckers as an integral part of our work. We must end this rebellion against the holy order of nature! The peace activist must be a systems shaman who brings into conjunction science, spirituality, healing, justice, ecology, economy, security, and all those other spokes that will turn the great wheel of peace. Vandana Shiva is an example of such an ambassador of peace. Based in Delhi, Shiva weaves together several of those spokes in the peace wheel. Trained as a physicist, she also completed a doctorate in philosophy. But rather than remain in academia as a scientist and philosopher, she has applied herself to addressing food and ecology issues in the global South and in India. She is a leading women's rights advocate and a brilliant critic of the aspects of globalization that have damaged the economies of poorer nations. She also links spirituality and activism and Vedic mysticism and ecology. Her website describes her latest organization and its philosophy:

Navdanya International, founded in India by physicist and internationally renowned activist Dr. Vandana Shiva, was born out of a vision of peace and non-violence. Navdanya's aim is to defend and protect nature and the rights of people access to food and water and dignified jobs and livelihoods. Promoting local and ecological food models is critical to alleviating poverty, hunger, and safeguarding natural resources, including water, especially in this time of climate change chaos. Articulating rarely heard views from the global South, Navdanya believes that cultural and biological diversity is essential for ensuring creative, peaceful societies throughout the planet.[2]

Simple rules for complex systems

Another great ambassador of peace is Louise Diamond.[3] Louise is a visionary soul who has not shied away from promoting a whole-systems perspective to government policy makers. A founder of the Institute for Multi-Track Diplomacy, she also created Global Systems Initiatives as a way to promote systems thinking in Washington, DC. It was at a gathering of this group in Crystal City, Virginia, in 2007 that I was invited to join Louise and other systems thinkers in formulating approaches for policy makers to use in applying a systems perspective in their work. We developed twelve simple rules of systems thinking for complex global issues. While this list may sound a little rarefied and abstract, the approach can be concretized and oriented toward the enactment of new behaviors. Infrastructures of peace would emerge if these rules were put into action.

I have edited and in some cases reframed the rules we created and have added commentary oriented to the field of peacebuilding.

1. **In complex systems, all the elements or agents are interconnected and interdependent. What happens to one affects all others.** *Therefore connect the disconnected.*

For example, people who are illiterate have a hard time in contemporary societies: they experience frustration, isolation, and humiliation, and they find difficulty getting work. Some turn to crime because they simply cannot cope. If you connect this fact to the fact that a large number of illiterate people are in prison, you can see that investments in literacy programs might reduce the prison population and prevent some crime.

2. **Complexity is the nature of living systems. In complex systems, multiple agents combine and interact in unpredictable and nonlinear ways. This implies that any given decision can lead to unintended consequences. *Therefore ground yourself in unpredictability.***

Control freaks, please note that you only create systemic disruptions by not cooperating with flow and change. This is a call to practice nonattachment and to release when necessary. A fixation with making things predictable leads to *dead* certainty! Life is flow.

3. **In a web of interconnectedness, there are many nodes where agents meet. These interactions determine what will happen elsewhere in the system. The nature and quality of each interaction in one part of a system creates a paradigm for relating in other parts of the system. *Therefore create conditions for quality engagements at every level in the system.***

The peacebuilder is a systems shaman, always looking to optimize the quality of interactions between people as a way to lubricate the flow of relationships in the larger system. Nobel Peace laureates, such as Desmond Tutu, demonstrate the ability to forge strong bonds between many kinds of people and different strata of society. No relationships are inferior to others, and all relationships demand in their own way skillful and meaningful interactions. Great peace leaders know that there is no lesser being on the face of the earth.

4. **All living systems exchange energy and information across their boundaries. At any point, there can be imbalances or stuck places in these flows. *Therefore rebalance the flows across boundaries.***

This one is key: you may think there is nothing leaking between your boundary and that of someone whose values differ from your own, but that is precisely where things get stuck in the social body. This is where invisible walls are erected and the pretense of civility exists. When we create hard and fast *them* and *us* categories, we interrupt the flow across boundaries. This is where peace ambassadors commit to expanding their comfort zone to be more inclusive and where they find *the essential link* between themselves and others. Dialogue rebalances the flow.

5. **All living systems develop patterns that become self-reinforcing and difficult to change. In fractal geometry, we see how patterns recur at different scales.** *Therefore constantly repattern for the sustainability and well-being of the whole.*

Too many of our political and business leaders are myopic. They see only the pattern right under their noses. When those in the scientific, academic, and social activist community who are looking at larger patterns cry, "Cliff's edge approaching!" they are called alarmist by these same "leaders." Then when the edge is reached, someone else is always at fault. As human rights activists know well, it often takes the catastrophic deterioration of a situation before people recognize that they have been tracking the patterns that lead to genocide, ethnic cleansing, or systemic oppression.

Because everything is always in movement, it is essential to have an intention to serve the best interests of the dynamic, ever-evolving whole and to organize our behaviors around that intention. To claim that any system could survive if each part set out to optimize its exclusive self-interest is not even worthy of kindergarten logic, yet this idea persists as a sacred tenet of whole cadres of elites. As John Donne wrote centuries ago, "No man is an island, entire of itself; every man is a piece of the continent, a part of the main." Serve the whole!

6. **Living systems teach us that everything is a whole in itself and, at the same time, part of a larger whole.** *Therefore attend both to the smallest parts and the greatest wholes.*

We have been learning this one in the peace movement: do not go out and oppose war and then ignore the violence in your own neighborhood or your own family. Some peacebuilders have a way of diverting their attention from issues that call for their personal involvement. But when we avoid dealing with "the small stuff," it usually grows in significance. Folk and indigenous wisdom reminds us that authentic progress radiates out from the hearth and the home to the wider world. It is most honorable to seek to do the greatest good for the largest number of people, but in the end, our service to the greatest whole is compromised if we are not grounded in a practice that serves those around us.

7. **Living systems interact in a networked fashion. Networks decentralize the activity of the whole and add to its efficiency.** *Therefore pay attention to emerging networks.*

The planet is being wired around emerging social networks. These networks can spin webs of connectivity, gestate new ideas, and cast off outmoded concepts. They are clusters of self-organizing, like-minded individuals attracted to communicate and collaborate in a nonhierarchical fashion. These emerging networks create synergy around a multiplicity of concerns and social issues—as well as building virtual conviviality. They are increasingly beginning to influence the corporate mainstream media with memes of social participation and collaboration. The emerging planetary peace movement is gaining vital oxygen from the pluralistic nature of emerging social-cause-oriented networks and their accelerating dissemination of new templates in conscious business, philanthropy, and many other arenas of social transformation.

Governments bent on control and ideological uniformity seek to limit these emerging networks. Technological repression is still repression. And from an evolutionary perspective, repression equals regression. The Mubarak regime in Egypt learned to its dismay that cutting off Internet and cell phone access during the early days of the uprising drove people into the streets. Having communicated with one another about the need for change, they were not about to accept even further regression. Ironically, the regime moved many from being virtual activists to ones who showed up in the streets in unprecedented numbers.

One final point on emerging networks: we must recognize that the virtual world and the actual world need to meet. Virtual networks can gestate creative concepts, but people are needed to actualize those dreams. Pay attention to those emerging networks that not only share new ideas but also really live and embody them.

8. **Systems move between various degrees of stability and instability, order and disorder. When the disorder becomes too great, things fall apart. When the order is too rigid, things can't grow or develop. Instability is an aspect of chaos. A certain degree of instability, known as the edge of chaos, can be where creativity and innovation occur.** *Therefore do not fear chaos but use it to bring about greater coherence.*

A great deal is made about chaos by those who claim they are saving us from it. Those who want to cling to power have a tendency to stoke fear about anarchy: "Après moi le deluge" (after me, the deluge), said Louis XV.

But chaos arrives as a natural part of life's unpredictability; new conditions arise that can represent either the wrench in the works or the opportunity to create a better design. When we respond to changing conditions with a mind-set of learning and an openness to growth and greater possibility, we draw a new level of order out of the limitless open-ended possibilities of chaos. Breakdown may indeed be the prerequisite for breakthrough, unless of course you want to use breakdown to reinforce another version of the same old, same old. But as Ervin Laszlo points out in *The Chaos Point: The World at the Crossroads*, it is too late for a business-as-usual approach. He suggests that there are so many destabilizing elements—terrorism, climate change, nuclear proliferation, resource depletion, and so on—that we as a species cannot survive if we do not use this breakdown to self-actualize at a higher level of integration. From this perspective, chaos can provide us with a great evolutionary opportunity to design a high level of planetary order.

9. **All living systems exist in a single field where subtle influences can have large repercussions. Quantum physics suggests that even the so-called objective observer is an engaged participant.** *Therefore wherever you find yourself in any system, remember that you are a player.*

This concept in systems theory has been referred to as "the butterfly effect": the idea that small fluctuations in air currents can affect larger weather patterns.

I am reminded of the concept that God is a circle whose center is everywhere and whose circumference can never be found. In the field of existence, the center is everywhere. This suggests that a person's voice and the resonance it carries should never be discounted simply because that person stands alone. Being an ambassador of peace is about not only remembering that you are a player, and doing so with originality and audacity, but helping others to do so as well. To discount yourself or any other being is to swallow the poison of effacement. It is to deny that you are a representative of the whole and that wholeness is seeded in everything.

But let us remember we have no complete map of how the inner affects the outer. When Rosa Parks sat down and refused to be seated at the back of the bus, she had no idea how far the resonance of that one action would carry. When the young man walked in front of a line of tanks heading into Tiananmen Square, he had no idea that this action would become an image that inspired the democracy movement all over the world. Even today you can still Google that image and feel how it uplifts you to see the power of one human being. Peace is about inhabiting that power wherever you are—and letting the invisible process of subtle effects in the larger field of interactions follow its own course. It all begins from an inner impulse or a clear intention.

10. **The parts of a living system share a common purpose. That is what defines a system: parts operating with a common purpose. Purpose drives the energy of a system to achieve its goals.** *Therefore constantly reexamine goals and purposes for alignment with current needs and reality.*

Sometimes we wake up and discover that our life is heading in the wrong direction. We are doing everything right, but our original purpose is no longer relevant to us. We outgrow purpose. Here we need to be good synthesizers. It is all too easy to get into a frame where we are replacing or updating the parts but not attending to the relevance of the system and where it is taking us. If we do not do this regularly, we tend to move from one revolution to another or to succumb to fads and whims. The same can happen to a social system. One day, Eastern Europe woke up and decided that being part of the Communist bloc was no longer relevant; within a few months, it had liberated itself from Communist rule.

Sometimes we must take on the prophetic responsibility of those who look ahead and see where the current highway is heading. It is often hard to warn people when they see no reason not to perpetuate the system they have learned to survive or thrive in. But peace depends on those with prophetic vision and insight who show us the need to re-align our goals and purposes. One such prophet is David Korten, who for decades has not only warned us about corporate excess but also shown us how to create sustainable economies. Sometimes the needed course correction is a really big one!

11. **Living systems exist within unique conditions, which are the underlying context of the system. Human context is rooted in worldview, culture, and meaning.** *Therefore articulate your deepest belief and dialogue about contrasting versions of common narratives.*

If we don't dialogue, we end up with division. We start to suspect people's motives when we do not understand how they make meaning.

The evolution of meaning systems is a huge topic, but for peacebuilders one thing is clear: imposing one meaning system on another creates conflict and violence.

People have different ways of narrating the same thing. Take health, for example. One will say that health comes primarily from believing in God and obeying moral codes. Another will say that health is strictly related to diet and exercise and influenced by genetic factors. Yet another will say health is about balancing life goals, happiness, freedom, nutrition, and exercise as part of an approach to overall well-being. We gain so much more from the process of dialogue than attempts to bring a forced convergence of belief.

People who have dialogued about differences invariably agree that the process is not about changing their beliefs but rather about experiencing a ground of being in which they can feel safe to believe whatever they want to believe. Beliefs can shrink from their absolutist claims in the face of love and acceptance. The biggest challenge in peace work is not the practice of dialogue itself; it is getting people to the table where they can experience one another's humanity.

12. **Living systems are learning systems. Nature is based on an ecology of learning and adaptation set in motion by feedback from changing environments and new conditions.** *Therefore welcome feedback, and base learning on the fullest range of signals, messages, and inputs.*

The reason we can tend to resist feedback is that it can upset the status quo and require a change in behavior. Feedback can take many forms, and sometimes we develop a pattern of ignoring feedback from certain quarters.

The psychiatrist Judith Orloff has written that as a scientifically trained physician, she tended to listen to the rational mind and discount instinct. When she almost lost a patient in a suicide attempt because she ignored her intuition, she vowed to listen to the full range of inner and outer information at her disposal.

Much of our work is allowing feedback to arise in a mutually affirming environment. It is very difficult for people to receive feedback that is directed at them as if they were the problem or if it is presented as a judgment of who they are. No one can learn in an environment of hostility. The best feedback helps people draw their own conclusions.

A final note on systemic transformation

Some readers will be familiar with Spiral Dynamics, an important theory formulated by Clare Graves and elaborated on and applied in practice by Don Beck and Christopher Cowan.[4] The basic idea is that optimal development occurs when the values of simpler social and cultural structures are incorporated but transcended, resulting in structures that are more responsive to life conditions as those conditions become more complex. The theory is sometimes misrepresented as negating the value systems of less complex societies, such as those that are tribally based. But understood correctly, Spiral Dynamics looks at three elements: the value clusters (associated with stages of societal complexity) that arise from prevailing conditions, the shadow aspect of each stage of development, and the transformation of values as conditions change.

One can see parallels with Maslow's hierarchy of needs, Kohlberg's theory of moral development, and Piaget's developmental process in individuals. But Spiral Dynamics is a theory based on social psychology and the complex values interactions of groups, which are quite distinct from the individual's journey to cognitive flowering, moral maturity, and self-realization.

Spiral Dynamics recognizes that every positive value can have a shadow side: for example, the protecting and liberating warrior can become the brutal dominator, or the entrepreneur can become exploiter and environmental wrecker. The theory explains how a culture that has evolved basic religious tenets can get locked into dogma and rigid truth claims that can lead to exclusion and even violence toward those who do not agree with those tenets. But as a society grows in complexity, it moves from the imposition of religious or ideological truth to an affirmation of individual rights and freedoms, including support for success-driven entrepreneurial opportunity and the accomplishment of more advanced material goals. Then, at the next stage of evolution, value clusters that emphasize social responsibility and shared ecological stewardship arise as conditions call for a rebalancing of excessive individualism and materialism. But this stage is achieved when people feel individually empowered enough to move beyond restrictive affiliations to act on behalf of the whole.

What may be of particular interest in thinking about a planetary culture of peace is that Spiral Dynamics next envisions a leap of consciousness to an even more advanced stage, one that reflects whole-systems awareness and whole-person integral development.

Let us summarize. In the first tier, we move from survival bands to larger tribal affiliations, and from there we see the emergence of warrior classes and empires based on affirming a separate ego identity—what Spiral Dynamics refers to as the movement from kinship groups to power gods. The next movement in the evolutionary spiral is toward identification with authority, conformity, and moral purpose. Then as societal contexts begin to change, there is a movement from authority to autonomy and a new emphasis on individual success and materialist identity. The final phase of the first tier revolves around social networking, collective responsibility, harmony, and equality. The leap to the so-called second tier in Spiral Dynamics theory is marked by an awareness of a deep connection between the individual being and the collective being, between personal action and optimal whole-systems functioning. It maps the emergence of deep coherence between being and doing and inner and outer—which is the territory of peace.

One cannot do justice to a complex and well-developed theory in a few paragraphs; what is of special interest here is the idea that to do peace work, you need to recognize where people are in their social and cultural evolution, and not where you would like them to be. Once you do that, you can speak to them within the highest positive values of their current cultural environment, so that you can prepare them for progressing to the next stage of development. Beck and Cowan coined the phrase "the spiral wizard" to refer to a person who is able to recognize and dialogue with any value system. This is the kind of fluency necessary for peace work.

Once you know the language of systems theories of this sort, you will be able to map how social transformation occurs. You do not need to don the wizard's hat, but you may want to grab an opportunity to spend time with a master teacher.

And who knows, you might even be able to not only hear *but also interpret* the word of the Lord!

THE
Call

You are called to make every point of contact with others a quality connection. Everything counts in our quest to humanize the world. Never underestimate small interventions to remove blockages between yourself and another, for in a world of inter-connections you never know what difference it will make.

Recognize the reality that even when we think we see the whole, we have a partial view. This should help you embody sufficient humility to examine contrasting perceptions even when you think you have a clear picture.

In a world that resonates with change from both inner and outer realities, know that you can constantly step up your game in new ways, from honing the clarity of your intentions to improving the skillfulness of your service to others. Practicing mindfulness, generosity of spirit, forgiveness, and gratitude will affect those around you, and taking action to make the world more tolerant, just, and sustainable will deepen your own inner life. The universe is designed such that when you play the field from inside out and from outside in, you become a representative of wholeness. Playing it only one way blocks you from gaining the feedback and growth so necessary for a conscious change agent.

What is called for more than ever is integration—not passivity and not zealotry. From a whole-systems perspective, you can no longer say that focusing everything on your spiritual development while the world around you goes into a deepening crisis is a balanced approach. Nor can you claim that putting all your energy into external problems and pursuing what I call burnout activism is as virtuous as it may seem. Peace is an integral practice.

Release, release, release! Whatever you hold on to that you need to let go will end up hurting you.

The ultimate damage after breakdown or injury is to stay damaged. Maybe what is blocking you is something inside that requires releasing an old enmity, guilt, or sense of inadequacy, or maybe it is a truth you need to face. Equally, the blockage may be someone who gets power from standing in your way. Sometimes we have to move toward the things that block us and really engage them before they will release.

Letting go requires letting go of fear. Fear has a way of submerging itself. When you are looking for what is holding you back and you seek to know the source of the problem, fear is often the source of that mechanical and artificial "what problem?"

Think of the healthy exercise of power as releasing flow in a system that has become compromised or backed up as a result of accumulating blockage. True power is never domination but the increase of flow in service to the whole. Never be afraid to be powerful when you understand this.

Sometimes the feedback you receive is uncomfortable, sometimes it may be inaccurate, but it is always worthy of your consideration. If it has no value or nutrition, let it pass through; if it has some merit, digest it.

We get feedback in multiple ways. In an unpredictable and changing world, the feedback comes when circumstances change and we see what we have been steadfastly ignoring.

Tune in to change, for it is the bearer of messages that must be responded to. Some people spend a lifetime managing conditions around them and living an elaborate illusion of control only to find that they have blocked the feedback that tried to let them know they were inhibiting their own most essential qualities.

Only by tuning in to your essence can you release all that will hold you back if you don't let go. And if you don't let go, chaos may erupt to get your attention or to offer you a chance to find a whole new order and meaning in your life.

Reflection AND Practice

We live in an era when we are tilting toward greater chaos. If we do not begin to reverse climate change, resource depletion, unsustainable consumption patterns, war, weapons proliferation, and egregious human rights violations, we could rapidly devolve as a species. Yet the edge of chaos opens up great possibilities.

Our breakthroughs are fed by taking the best of the past and discarding its dysfunctions. New possibilities sometimes emerge out of bold originality, but they are more often than not a creative synthesis of past and present aligned toward a better future. What are you doing to transform the aspects of chaos you see unfolding in the world? What are you doing to reinforce the note that you are a player and not just a passive observer? Project yourself to the end of your life and look back: what will be one arena where you sustained your passion and creativity to make a difference? Remember, you have the goods to make a difference. But avoid trying to play too many places in the field; people are already frenetic and too busy. Remember that one of the instructions to influence complex systems is about focusing on quality interactions. Look around at any system you want to influence and determine where you can have the most strategic impact by upgrading the quality of your interactions. Change often begins when one pivotal relationship is changed.

For each of the twelve rules for complex systems, I suggest a practice. Review them with an eye to seeing how you can apply each one in your workplace or community. Could you form a discussion group? There is a lot to master in getting clear about the systems concept and the recommended action to take.

Systems theory was influenced by meteorology. Weather systems reveal how small shifts in a weather pattern can affect the formation of larger storms. Hence, the idea that a butterfly flapping its wings can create a cascading series of effects leading to a mighty wind. That is a caricature, but the principle holds through. Ask any navigator, who will quickly affirm that very slight directional shifts can lead you way off course, sometimes with disastrous consequences.

This reminds us that we don't have to take on everything: we can be more strategic. Where in your own contribution would you have the most influence for the least effort? People often say they are too busy for peace work. When I ask them about their lives, they say they are in the school PTA, they spend time on Facebook, or they run a small business. My point is that creating a culture of peace is not about going off and doing separate peace activities; it is about bringing the peace agenda inside systems. If you are in the PTA, why not promote teaching empathy, which is known to reduce violence? Why not learn about HeartMath's brilliant work and bring it to your school? Maybe you can use Facebook, as many do, to promote a cause that you dedicate yourself to or even post a YouTube clip about it. If you run a small business, you have choices to make with regard to sustainability, conscious business, and enlightened labor practices. The important thing is to experiment as an individual with influencing a larger audience or system.

So start with where you are and see where you can have the greatest impact on a larger system. You may be surprised to see that you have more influence than you imagined and that you are the Trojan horse of peace already inside the gates. But instead of attacking, your assignment is to bring healing.

Another important theme in mastering systems thinking is the notion of perspective. What you are looking at often relates to where you are looking from. Be rigorous in asking yourself from what part of a system you are evaluating or critiquing that system. Partial stories get us nowhere. Nothing is more demanding than truth, for truth is informed by contrasting perspectives and by knowledge about the relationships between parts and the whole.

Peace requires a deeply sustained commitment to truth process, which means integrating various perspectives until they align with a greater truth or until they dissolve in the reality of a greater truth. Throughout this book, you are discovering that peace is not possible without truth but also that peace work is not a matter of bringing truth to people or hammering down their doors about the lies they live. Rather, it is *truth process* that brings us to *experiences* of truth. Truth process is fearless, compassionate, sensitive, subtle, and uncompromising. How we collectively experience more encompassing truth will define how creatively we evolve the peace movement and will eventually determine just how effective we become as systems shamans, transforming cultures by harvesting their own highest meaning.

Chapter 10

~

The 21st-Century Peace Ambassador as Evolutionary Leader

A s we evolve, we become more conscious of consciousness. We become more self-reflective. We explore inner reality, as well as the way everything outside us manifests its own qualities and capacities. And we begin to develop subtle capacities and to exercise conscious choices to cultivate wisdom and compassion. Eventually, as we meet changing conditions and challenges, we move toward an understanding of universal responsibility. More and more, we as individuals come into resonance with the collective; each of us plays a greater role in actualizing the potential of the whole. But as I have argued in this book, we are unfortunately still fitfully emerging from structures where individuality has either been repressed or overindulged, where the relation of the individual to the whole is profoundly out of balance.

Evolution allows for all kinds of experimentation in order to find that balance, but in the end it optimizes for the survival of the fittest. For a while the fittest may appear to be the most voracious, but it turns out that the fittest are not usually the most self-serving and competitive but the most skillful collaborators and creative adapters. Those who learn how to optimize conditions for an abundant diversity of life shall inherit the earth.

We humans are learning a very hard lesson and having to learn it fast. The dinosaurs were around a lot longer than us, and they became extinct because they couldn't adapt. Our lesson now is to learn how to adapt in ways that creatively serve the whole while supporting the authentic needs of the individual. Humans have too often flourished at the expense of the whole. And in case you hadn't noticed, nature is telling us to adapt more skillfully, sustainably, and peacefully, or it will rebalance—with catastrophic consequences for human life. After all, without the current human activity, planet Earth would cleanse its oceans, clean its air, regrow its forests, and cool its overheating atmosphere. No doubt the loss of species diversity would also be turned around.

The day has gone when a few bold leaders could lead us out of this mess. It is not clear that our current political leaders are hearing nature's siren: "Warning! Failure to adapt." If they are consciously ignoring it, they should be regarded in the same way we view those who commit crimes against humanity. If we could do anything to avoid destroying our planet, shouldn't that be a priority?

Here is an analogy: You take your child to school, and the principal says, "We have electrical problems, and there is a 75 percent chance that these problems will cause a fire. But don't worry; we won't let little Jenny get burned." If your response is polite, you might say, "I think I'll take my child home. Let me know when you have dealt with the electrical problems." If any children went into that school and a fire broke out, the principal would be held criminally liable. Even if he said there was only a 10 percent chance of fire, no one in their right mind would send a child into that school. To be truly safe, the chance would have to be as unlikely as a fire being started by a bolt of lightning. So draw your own conclusions about the inaction of government leaders regarding climate change and the loss of life that will occur as a result. Even though they have been warned, and warned by the vast majority of the planet's climate scientists, they refuse to act decisively. Only a new kind of leadership will save the day!

How, you may ask, is climate change a problem for peacebuilders? I was at a meeting in Washington, DC, on systems thinking and policy change in 2009. Two military representatives of the Joint Chiefs were present. They outlined various scenarios of war, conflict, and mass refugee movements arising out of climate change catastrophes. When the military is drawing up scenarios, you know the situation is serious. But it seems world leaders are waiting to see who will have the courage to do something first.

We noted in the chapter on systems thinking how peace is interconnected with poverty, women's rights, a healthy democracy, social networks, and so on. I have particularly stressed that peace calls us to cultivate capacities in compassionate and skillful listening, nonviolent communication, truth telling, forgiveness, and reconciliation. Without these qualities we cannot move the entire social order to the next turn in the spiral of our collective evolution.

As brilliant peacebuilders, Lynne and Bill Twist founded the Pachamama Alliance to help the Achuar people save their rain forest territory in Ecuador.[1] The Achuar people in their wisdom told them that the most urgent priority was for them to *change the dream of the West*. In other words, the world cannot have peace unless *we* change our ways. Saving the rain forests and protecting indigenous lifestyles require those who live in advanced materialist societies to dream a new dream of communal well-being and sustainability. It is obvious that we urgently need legions of awakened and conscious new-paradigm evolutionary leaders, who can rise to the occasion as we face the challenges left by distorted, myopic leadership.

Characteristics of today's emerging peace ambassadors

Here are some of the defining traits and qualities of the emerging leaders devoted to cultivating peace:

They experience a hologram of the whole

We know that the right hemisphere of the brain is able to see whole pictures. It can leap from seeing the elements themselves to experiencing how they connect and what happens when they do. We honor the left brain because it can analyze, and we honor the right brain because it can synthesize. This capacity to experience the "patterns that connect"—as if they come together like light beams in a three-dimensional hologram—is vital for any leader. Indeed, while others may get lost in the details, leaders must be able to see the overall design. Here, I am not suggesting that leaders have all the answers but rather that they—at minimum—must be able to initiate dialogue that leads to insights into how we can serve what physicist and systems theorist Fritjof Capra refers to as the whole "web of life."

The whole can also be experienced in a deeply sensorial way: the holographic vision is felt at the level of gut instinct, in the emotional field of the heart's knowing, and in the mind's intellectual lucidity.

They are servants of the whole

"Serving the whole" refers to the capacity to commit to a vision or, as some would say, surrender to it. There is no hedging. Nor is there any need for "I've got the answer" bravado. Serving the whole requires spiritual maturity, for one of the major aspects of surrender is letting go of ego. The servant of the whole cannot be what we have called a partisan of the part. Leadership is greatly compromised when it is not supported to fulfill this function of serving the whole.

They see problems from the perspective of solutions

With any problem, we want to know who is responsible or often who is to blame for creating it. We can get sucked into problems, and they can shape our thinking in ways that keep us preoccupied with what is wrong rather than on creating solutions.

Problems can quickly progress from warning signal to entropy zone, where they start to pull down everything that surrounds them. Naturally, problems demand attention, but the challenge is not to allow our attention to be framed or defined by them. The solution does not lie inside the problem, but it does require understanding and accepting the gravity of the problem.

The leader who sees the big picture focuses attention on the solution that picture offers. Any new problems that arise are indicators that the journey to the solution is going astray. The mature leader keeps attention on the desired outcome and allows problems to be learning signposts. It is a matter of seeing where energy is diverted and making sure more energy is not poured into the diversion but into the course correction. The desired outcome must always be the strongest attractor or the evolutionary lure.

They welcome all forms of feedback

Because everything is in movement, it is a mistake to believe that any given path to the accomplishment of a vision will be secured or guaranteed. Zealots get attached to a "this is the only way" orientation. The evolving leader, immersed in visionary insight, does not get locked into a particular strategy. The nineteenth-century British politician William Wilberforce experienced a vision of the end of slavery and surrendered to it, but he spent a lifetime experimenting with different strategies and tactics to reach that goal. All his efforts had a cumulative effect, but in the end clever parliamentary process played the decisive role.

Because the emerging leader's energy stays inside visionary goals, feedback is welcomed rather than regarded as negative or obstructive. This is the stance of a highly dedicated learner whose true passion is the acquisition of knowledge that advances human evolution rather than of skills to broker on the market. What emerges is a dynamic combination of being led by vision and being grounded in the reality of what is.

They are not defeated by petty or cynical obstruction

We noted earlier that the cynic disguised as the voice of reason constantly finds objections to an idealist's course of action. Multiple stakeholders with a vested interest in the status quo will offer all kinds of "practical" reasons why things should be delayed or done differently.

"But you haven't thought of . . . " or "You really have no idea what you are getting yourself into!" These are the nattering nabobs of negativity. But oh, how they can present themselves insidiously as quite reasonable! "You really need to get grounded," they say. Translation: you are not protecting your own narrow self-interest, or you are about to tread on their self-interest.

But the leader who has inhabited a vision of the solution won't be deterred by these voices. One of the hallmarks of conscious and peaceful leaders is that they are able to smoke out the difference between genuine feedback and cynical posturing. When you have surrendered to something great, you are not so likely to be deterred by petty objections. Your steadfast commitment to your life's purpose frees your heart and mind to experience an inner peace that doesn't fall prey to worry or short-term thinking.

They cultivate multiple ways of knowing

The evolving leader is moving into a space where mentally focused intelligence alone cannot serve. We are called to integrate the instinctual intelligence of the gut, the spacious inclusiveness of the heart, and the lucidity of the mind. In recent years, science has explored these distributed intelligences in the body, and new research in psychology and consciousness studies has given us maps of a new human wholeness.[2] Departing widely from the typical reductionism of most mainstream research, the new curriculum emerging out of a collaboration between science, psychology, and spirituality points at expanded human capacities.

They value the role of compassion

I once sat down for tea with the commander and president of the West Point Military Academy. He told me that he taught a class on leadership, and at the beginning and end of the class, he asked cadets to list ten qualities of a great military leader, in order of importance. By the time they completed his class, many understood that the most important quality was compassion or empathy. The students understood that a good soldier was one who was dedicated to protecting life, not destroying it.

We have discovered that empathy is a root intelligence affecting others and that a whole array of qualities of emotional intelligence can be cultivated. Cultivating an advanced emotional and social intelligence is only possible when those who teach such intelligence have themselves mastered it. When our leaders mirror emotional and social intelligence, it percolates through institutions, transforming them from the inside out.

The evolution of our species calls for deep relational maturity, for without it we will never know peace.

They move in an amplified field

When leaders are living a full commitment to their ideals and manifesting their essential qualities, they live in an amplified field of being. In their presence, we feel richer and more expanded. They model for us the courage and the commitment to be true to ourselves.

This amplified field is magnanimous and not compromised by any suggestion of meanness or rivalry. In fact, evolved leaders are always creating a space for others to evolve along with them. In some traditions, they say you need to meet a spiritual master so that you can experience the expanded state he or she lives in. Indeed, it does help to see the leadership you aspire to actualized and embodied. It catalyzes your growth to be invited into your own creativity and greatness by leaders who have stepped into theirs.

I have personally experienced this as a miraculous sense of flow, connection, and synchronicity. When I am in the presence of an amplified being, I move out of staccato and into flow. For truly great beings, there is no disruption of the flow, no matter what happens around them.

They cooperate with the great mystery

Once you cross the threshold of ego-dominated personality and reach deeper into the source of your consciousness, you touch a great mystery. Getting to this place is clearly a spiritual aspect of leadership.

Mystery opens us to experience aspects of reality for which we have no reference points. In recent years, we have seen both scientists and mystics acknowledge this sense of the mystery of life and existence. For example, the astronaut Edgar Mitchell spoke widely about experiencing a mystical sense of oneness with everything in creation as he journeyed back to Earth after walking on the moon. This does not mean that he disconnected from the reality of his space capsule; it means he was connected to a comprehensive reality beyond rational explanation.

Mystical teachings of the world's religions, as well as most indigenous traditions, say it is important to cultivate a relationship to mystery, sometimes referred to as the great mystery. Generally, they teach that encountering mystery has the power to wash away false certainty and rigidity. It cleanses us of a conditioned mind and any notions of self-importance. "The most beautiful thing we can experience is the mysterious," Einstein said. "It is the source of all great art and all science."

When we commune with the mysterious, we get a taste of the unity of all life and are graced with hints and flashes of reality's grand design. The great mystery is always pulsing with both emptiness and fullness. Cooperating with it is the essence of great leadership.

They avoid judgmental thoughts and feelings

There is a difference between being discerning and being judgmental. Every leader needs to be highly discerning about people, proposals, and situations. Discerning truth from lies and the real from the fake are prerequisites of good leadership. Discernment frees us up for what is essential.

Being merely judgmental carries freight. It is loaded with divisive condemnation and moral superiority. It is often concerned with being right or being seen to be right. Standing in judgment of others is a way of placing yourself above them. It is one thing to judge a person's actions, but it is quite another to judge that person at the level of their being.

We drown in a sea of negativity when we put ourselves above others. It is impossible for us to lead if we regard others as inferior. The way an evolved and peaceful leader removes the virus of judgmental thinking and feeling is to constantly promote an atmosphere where people give and receive healthy feedback.

They witness the best in others

More than anything else we all have a need to be seen. Those who recognize our essential qualities are the true peacebuilders: they let us know that they see the significance of our lives. Meanness of spirit stems from a place of neglect and the absence of nurturance and love. When we have not been seen and loved for who we are, we can turn sour and even violent.

The peaceful leader is sourced by the power of love. Love is solar; it radiates. It shares of itself. This generosity is not threatened by others' strengths and qualities; on the contrary, it draws them out. Ultimately, it draws out the essence in the other because it speaks from essence to essence.

This leadership quality contains a balance of both feminine and masculine; think of combining the safety and acceptance of the feminine ground of being with the masculine energy of "Try harder—I know you have it in you to do better." When we see the best in others, we are seeing them as they are, as well as seeing their true potential. Imagine how quickly the world would be transformed if we all developed the capacity to see the best in one another and understood that when we do the opposite, we breed hostility.

They step into authentic power

Leadership is the consummate skill of handling power with grace on behalf of the greater good. The conscious and peaceful leader knows that power is never stolen from others. The abuse of power results from a deeply rooted inner sense of inadequacy in the abusive leader. When power is distorted, the leader unconsciously conceals this place of inadequacy and heavily camouflages it so no one can identify it. Ironically, violent leaders first process their own energy through a pattern of subversion, repression, and denial in themselves long before their power manifests in the distorted way they treat others. When asked about the slaughter of nonviolent protesters in his country, President Assad of Syria replied softly, "But I would never kill my own people." Assad is guilty of deep denial, but there are other, equally dangerous syndromes, especially that of projection. For example, in so many places of the violent abuse of power that I have visited, imbalanced leaders create an atmosphere where enemies are essential, where their opponents are labeled as dogs, rats, cockroaches, foreigners, fanatics, or terrorists. Inauthentic leadership always resorts to some form of name-calling so that it can stand above what is below.

As I have pointed out repeatedly in this book, authentic power is always shared and always facilitates the empowerment of others. Power is the flow of energy that enables other energies to gather, connect, and move conditions toward desired outcomes. Authentic power can never take an approach where the ends justify the means. To be authentic, power must always justify the means to any end goal. In fact, the process must mirror the summoning and engagement of the highest values, not the lowest common denominator. The one who has the power to empower others is an authentic peace ambassador.

But let's be clear: we are talking about how to ramp up power, not level it off. We are called to mobilize a whole-systems transformation, and that will require mass empowerment. We must get out of the way of the great power of our own evolutionary potential and stop blocking our destiny with insanely petty power games.

They skillfully transmute adversity

Leadership is defined by how it deals with adversity. When we confront serious challenges, we reveal our qualities and capacities at a deeper level, and usually our baggage is also revealed. Everything we haven't been dealing with is discharged. At the same time, our core strengths are summoned.

A transformational leader embodies a consciousness that can stand in the fire of gross animosity and transmute it into compassion, forgiveness, and a willingness to face fear. We reveal so much when we are tested. As I pointed out in chapter 6, transmuting adversity calls for a commitment to doing no harm to those who oppose you, if that is possible. It even means doing everything in your power to protect them from their own unskillful actions. It takes great skill to make sure that someone else's lack of skill does not trigger your own. It is precisely in a time of adversity that we can be pulled back into old wounds—for negativity can open those old wounds like nothing else.

They do not sell cheap remedies

Our frequent embrace of simplistic solutions would be almost endearing if that tendency did not lead to so many dead ends. Shallow, quick-fix, feel-good solutions abound. We confuse the truly miraculous with cynically marketed overnight cures. Demagogues are always touting simplistic solutions or framing issues in terms of good guys and bad guys. Nuance and subtlety are thrown out in favor of exaggerated certainty.

Complexity need not make things confusing. It can highlight webs of connection and the need for greater inclusion in assessing problems and designing solutions. The peaceful leader is not motivated by false imperatives or premature solutions.

Humility does not need to claim the answer to every question because it knows that knowledge comes from wrestling with doubt and understanding dissent. Combine power, humility, and authenticity, and you have the antidote to cheap remedies and snake oil.

They collaborate and unite

Since the new-paradigm leader is not an enforcer, the ability to foster collaboration is the key to effective service. To inspire collaboration, the leader needs to energize others with a clear vision and help them feel empowered to be part of realizing its accomplishment.

In our individualistic postmodern society, collaboration is something we are still very much learning about. We learn aspects of collaboration at home, in the office, and in team sports. We collaborate here and there but not necessarily as a way of life. What seems to be missing is the kind of learning that stretches our capacity for exploring collaborative models of development. Indigenous ways of supporting kinship groups and tribal affiliations have much to teach us, but we need balance. I have encountered indigenous communities where the community breathes as one but where often individuals leave to explore their unique identity. Our evolving story as a species seems to want us to learn how we can integrate both unique individual and collective identities.

Uniting people in a common vision requires emerging leaders to understand how unity and diversity are part of living-systems design. We are brought together by those who can show us how to live principles that honor diversity and yet intensify a common purpose. The peaceful leader helps open up common ground, not so everyone sings from the same song sheet but so they can discover a harmony never experienced before.

This new form of spacious and inclusive unity is the cornerstone of the emerging planetary peace movement. It has room for multiple forms of leadership. In fact, the movement has left in the dust of evolutionary process any idea of a single model when it comes to leadership. The unimaginable is really happening: "We the people" are the voice of a new plateau of morality and shared higher consciousness.

As I write this in mid-2012, I look over the past year at the pain that people in the Middle East have endured to depose their dictators. Their passion to secure democracy for themselves and their children is evidence of the inexorable journey toward peace that so-called average people the world over are willing to give their lives to attain. And, frankly, the lords of ego just don't seem to understand how we can be evolving so fast—maybe because ego can make us tone deaf to the great longing for peace that resonates deep within the human soul and because it is baffled by the emergence of collective leadership.

THE
Call

If you think that these qualities of peaceful leaders are describing others, please take another look at them in relation to what is emerging in you. Let these qualities and capacities call you to embody them in your own context.

The pace of evolutionary change has kicked up as we approach a massive phase change from ego-dominated growth and leadership to greater psychological maturity and spiritual insight. You are not just a replaceable cog in the wheel of mechanistic progress. What is shaping our progress is nonlinear dynamics; everything is interrelated and connected. As we explored in the previous chapter, this means that small inputs can have large consequences, and a change in the part corresponds to a change in the whole. So, more than ever, this is the time to play your part.

You are called to tap into your essence and to make it your practice to speak to the essence of others. Unproductive conflict thrives on making peripheral differences seem like do-or-die core issues.

Resolve any significant hesitancy about your own leadership. You must cross the threshold of your own fears and inhibitions. If you really understood what is at stake, you would. You would immediately see how you could contribute. It is your ego that prevents you from taking action and from letting your authentic voice rise out of the ground of your own being. Equally, it is your ego that overcompensates when you have hesitated too long, leading you to make grandiose claims or gestures. The universe has hidden a secret in you. It is your job to reveal it.

The great mystery is an ally. It has nothing to do with your fear about what might go wrong in your life. It offers you a relationship with possibilities you cannot see or imagine. It loosens the grip of the grasping mind and controlling habits. It invites the deepest trust in what is unfolding. It calls you to collaborate with a vast design you cannot comprehend from a limited individualistic perspective. Let yourself be washed by the great mystery, and you will find, mysteriously, that you will have more knowing and guidance than you thought possible.

Do not allow yourself to be defeated by linear objections or obstructions. The world is turned upside down when the lesser rules the greater, and all kinds of moral and social disorder come when this happens. The cynic is a chameleon who shape-shifts to obstruct your core idealism. Don't fall for the cynic's diversionary ploys. And if the obstruction comes with a bullying tone, you might want to recall the suggestions for dealing compassionately, and effectively, with bullies.

Stand in your power. Yes, that means dispelling any heavily conditioned ideas you have about power. Authentic power is something that is allowed, not something that is either coerced or puffed up. Standing in your power is like opening the spigot of truth and creativity. It is about entering the flow of healing. We all learn as children that we have the power to obstruct; it is a quieter form of tantrum. But obstructionism in an adult is false power. True power facilitates.

You will know when you are really standing in your power by the flow of empowerment around you. More than anything else, your work as an ambassador of peace is about redefining power. Be integral. Know how to be vulnerable and confident, open and directive, firm and supple.

Reflection AND Practice

Thinking about leadership is undergoing a great revision. It entails a major worldview transformation and requires us to map distributive rather than concentrated leadership. There is a lot of work to do. We are called to dismantle old power and control hierarchies that have a vested interest in maintaining the status quo. Let's just say they won't go without a fight. They are good at shape-shifting appearances: the monarch leaves the throne only to be replaced with a slightly different version of someone sitting in the seat of concentrated power.

At the same time, we know that conscious people all across the planet are stepping up and demanding a greater role in shaping their societies. We are seeing passive electorates reengage as never before and with greater competencies to facilitate positive change. Revolution is now conscious evolution.

How are you summoning your own personal leadership? Where is your front line of engagement? Sometimes it is helpful to ask others for feedback. Sit down with a friend or two and ask them how they see your level of engagement in the world. Remember, a strong leader invites feedback. This is also good to do in a small group of colleagues where deep trust has been established.

Leadership invariably involves initiative. Sometimes initiating a shift in your pattern of relating to authority is a bold beginning. You stop displacing your innate authority and make a decision to stop projecting power and authority onto others. The energy that was projected is allowed to form as inner strength. You trust your feelings. You activate a deeper whole-body awareness. Your confidence develops from testing your strength and power as you cross threshold after threshold of fear or of your sense of inadequacy with centered vitality and composure.

Rediscovering how your body's intelligence is distributed and not centralized in just your head or your heart or your gut or your genitalia or your muscles but through the life of trillions of cells and the body's well-orchestrated electro- and biochemical responses—all this can reinforce different aspects of a whole-body wisdom.

Look for the undercultivated areas of your mind-body intelligence and develop them. If you are very "heady," work on listening to your enteric nervous system—your intuitive gut knowing. If you are overemotional, practice combining more intense physical activity with more rigorous mental challenges. If you are too alpha busy, balance yourself with a meditative spiritual practice. If you are too absorbed in the computer world, go out into nature regularly. We have emphasized that cultivating peace requires an integral approach and conscious attention to honing multiple ways of knowing.

Enough of imbalanced and unhealthy leadership! Be one of the emerging leaders whose doing reflects their being.

Some readers may be familiar with the astrological concept of Saturn as the representative of the force in the universe that rewards us when we carry out our essential life assignments. Saturn returns at various phases in our life to help us see whether we are on track with our deeper life's purpose. The reward for doing our homework is not smug self-satisfaction but an inner sense of fulfillment and completion. Mystics might call it tasting wholeness. Some think of this as a process of purification as we learn to live more and more in essence. When you can lead from this place, from the center of your being, you will be truly authentic. But don't equate this to some kind of perpetually mellow state, for if it is authentic and will carry the full range of your passion and purpose.

Review each of the qualities and attributes of peaceful leaders described in this chapter. Be linear if you like and privately rate yourself on a scale of one to ten for each leadership attribute. What is your profile? Where are your strengths and weaknesses? Now you know where you have homework to do.

Positive psychology teaches us that it is good to speak to the subconscious mind, with its worries and doubts, by creating strategic affirmations. Once you have completed your review, create a set of affirmations that boldly invite you to step into the qualities of a peaceful leader. Get creative. Affirm who you really know yourself to be in your essence.

Conclusion

Every good story has a denouement, when the hidden axis of the plot is revealed. But the human story is not a singular story: there is no single "Aha, that's what it was about!" moment. Ours is not a linear narrative of historical events—and when it is presented in that way, we know that it is someone's unique version of the tapestry of life. We are at once part of a dynamic and unfolding cosmic story and at the same time participants in a planetary story that is both tragic and comic, intimate and alienated, absurd and epic, individual and collective. We get to participate as a fractal on every level, from the infinite to the infinitesimal.

To be human is to be called to meet every existential challenge. None of us escapes the crucible of existence, though the intensity of its fire can vary dramatically in any given lifetime. Each human life is a reality that is asked to reveal its truth and that is invited to be a creative force in the lives of others. There is no lesser human being. No life is inconsequential. Even when we have no idea what power has summoned us into consciousness and moral choice, no living soul can sidestep that reality.

What is so brilliant and exciting about this phase of the human story is the visceral shock of awakening to the moment in the narrative when this greater truth of our sacred interdependence and oneness can be deeply realized by billions of people. We see the great wounds that have held us captive to notions of superiority and inferiority. We see everywhere the damage done by disrespect. We see the power that gorges on our vulnerability and that ever claws its way to domination. Yet we awake as it devolves. We arise in coherence as it declines into chaos. We claim the common ground of peace even as it fights for the exclusive rights of brutal or demeaning exploitation.

Yet we are not the victors, and there can be no vanquished in this story. We wake up to realize that we are the food that sustains the systems that oppress us. We are, in part, inside the belly of the beast we would overcome. We are the consumers who are the cause of Earth's frenzied destruction, as forests crash, species die off, and toxins saturate land, air, and sea. But we are awakening to the fact that we can change that story from inside this vast system of damage by changing the way we live, the way we eat, and the way we relate to one another. We can wean the system of its addictions by choosing a kind of vitality and health that is born of visionary knowledge, creative innovation, and the waveform of new communal behavior.

But if we are partly inside the belly of the self-devouring beast of greed and power intoxication, the new map of consciousness tells us that we are also partly outside it. As we evolve in conscious awareness, we see that we have a faculty that steps outside of ourselves and empowers us to self-witness. We are endowed with a self-reflective awareness. We can hold ourselves up and look into a great mirror to witness who it is we really are. We can shift from form to essence, from appearance to substance, and from illusion to reality.

We have the power to affirm what is true and deny what is false. What begins as simple moral choice flowers into a mature moral imagination. We move from the training wheels of right and wrong to honing wisdom and power, to giving energy and support to life-affirming and life-enhancing ways of being, and to withdrawing power from that which is unjust and unsustainable.

From inside the belly of the beast and from outside its limited awareness, peace has found a way to transform what is and to create new forms from the pure potential of consciousness itself. Holding fast to this integral path is the new discipline of peace.

There can never be peace when some are damned for the cruelty and injustice they ingested from the environment around them. There can never be peace as long as we are looking for scapegoats. Peace is the healer, not the triumphant conqueror. Peace goes to the places of our deepest wounding and brings the consciousness of love and compassionate connection to that which was separated from the whole.

The beauty of this moment in our collective experience is emerging into greater wholeness and lends itself to greater planetary connectivity. Even as brutal antagonisms flare up in various places, their virally unskillful hatreds have no significant power to stunt our collective emergence. Peace has been weaving a net of inclusion, where all are asked to bring their creative gifts to a global conversation that is only just beginning.

There is nothing passive about this process. Your voice can sparkle even in a conversation that includes many voices and diverse perspectives. Your voice can decidedly strengthen the weave of peace.

Hopefully, you have begun to see cynicism as a primary violation of your right to be. Let's not pretend that there are no immature voices asking you to be subservient to failure. They are asking you to tamp it down and knuckle under to blatantly adolescent power games. They are asking you to play what you now see is a losing game, a game that interrupts the momentum of our emancipation from the petty gods of material power and domination. You see the hysterical enticements of those willing to destroy the world itself in order to win the right to be at the top when all below are sinking. But you have evolved beyond these deadly games. And now your voice must scintillate with the truth of a vastly more enthralling use of our energy.

To change the collective story envisioned by planetary peace requires that each of us must learn to be more skillful in practicing all the manifold ways to peace. It should be abundantly clear that planetary peace requires more than a little nudge. It requires a great turnaround. It requires a massive shift in thinking, cultural conditioning, and the way we mobilize for change and transformation.

But you have come in time. You have been empowered to envision transformation on the scale that is needed. You have been given tools to connect with the whole world. You have been inducted into curricula that help you give voice to your heart's intelligence, your power to communicate nonviolently, your innate abilities to reconcile, forgive, and dialogue with difference and to engender new forms. You have been given the courage to step into the flow of tidal changes, where you will undoubtedly make an impact in ways you could hardly have imagined. You have been gestated in humanity's long journey to peace. You are an ambassador for all who have come before you, all who wrestled with oppression and who helped forge this vibrant moral imagination, which is now your richest inheritance.

Step into that very subtle power that is stronger than any coercive force. Dance in the complexity that will allow so many voices to find their own way to make global music without ever diminishing the beauty of uniquely local song. And when the children of the future walk in the garden of healing friendship and recover human balance with nature, they will bow to their ancestors who were known as the first ambassadors of global peace.

A final practice: visualize your own ancestors, going all the way back. Allow an uncensored version of their pain and struggle through deeply challenging conditions to be present for you in this moment. Now see future generations evolving to higher and higher forms of integration and skillful and harmonious relationship. Hold also those images. Now finally, see yourself in the midpoint between past and future. And smile. Smile all the way through. Smile as you acknowledge who you are in the story of peace.

And never lose that smile.

Notes

Chapter 1

1. See, for example, Walter de Gruyter's *International Journal of Humor Research*, published on behalf of the International Society of Humor Studies. Information on the biology of reward can be found in David P. Barash, *The Survival Game: How Game Theory Explains the Biology of Cooperation and Competition* (New York: Owl Books, Henry Holt, 2004) and Ralph Koster, *A Theory of Fun for Game Design* (Scottsdale, AZ: Paraglyph Press, 2005). For helpful background, see Daniel Goleman, *Social Intelligence: The Revolutionary New Science of Human Relationships* (New York: Bantam Dell, 2007).

Chapter 2

1. For more on shadow projections, see Carl Gustav Jung, *The Portable Jung* (New York: Penguin Books, 1971) and Deepak Chopra, Debbie Ford, and Marianne Williamson, *The Shadow Effect: Illuminating the Hidden Power of Your True Self* (Harper One, New York, 2010).

Chapter 3

1. To find out more about the Global Peace Index, visit the website of the Institute for Economics and Peace at http://www.economicsandpeace.org/.

2. To read the Earth Charter, go to
   http://www.earthcharterinaction.org/content/.
3. For a fuller discussion of Gurdjieff's theory of reciprocal maintenance,
   see J. G. Bennett, *Gurdjieff: Making a New World* (Santa Fe, NM:
   Bennett Books, 1992).
4. Frans de Waal, *The Age of Empathy: Nature's Lessons for a Kinder Society*
   (New York: Harmony Books, 2009); Jeremy Rifkin, *The Empathic
   Civilization: The Race to Global Consciousness in a World in Crisis*
   (New York: Jeremy P. Tarcher/Penguin, 2009).

Chapter 4
1. For more on Father Michael Lapsley's work,
   see http://www.healing-memories.org/.
2. To follow Jim Gordon's important work on international trauma
   recovery, go to http://www.cmbm.org/.

Chapter 5
1. More information on the groundbreaking work of the Institute of
   HeartMath can be found at http://www.heartmath.org/.
2. For a technical discussion of the amygdala's role in listening, see M.
   Wallentin et al., "Amygdala and heart rate variability responses from
   listening to emotionally intense parts of a story," *Neuroimage* 58, no. 3
   (October 2011): 963–73.
3. For some edgy science on the enteric nervous system, intuition, and the
   gut response, see Dean Radin, *Entangled Minds: Extrasensory Experiences
   in a Quantum Reality* (New York: Paraview Pocket Books, 2006).

Chapter 6
1. Nonie Sharp, *No Ordinary Judgment* (Canberra: Aboriginal Studies
   Press, 1996), p. 177.
2. Lederach is considered the leading authority on the concept of social
   healing. See John Paul Lederach and Angela Jill Lederach, *When
   Blood and Bones Cry Out: Journeys through the Soundscape of Healing and
   Reconciliation* (Queensland, Australia: University of Queensland Press,
   2010).

3. For a report on the observer effect in physics,
   see "Quantum Theory Demonstrated: Observation
   Affects Reality," *Science Daily*, February 27, 1998,
   http://www.sciencedaily.com/releases/1998/02/980227055013.htm.

Chapter 7

1. The Challenge Day website is at http://www.challengeday.org/.
2. For more about Marshall Rosenberg and nonviolent communication,
   see Marshall Rosenberg, *Nonviolent Communication: A Language of Life*
   (Encinitas, CA: PuddleDancer Press, 2003).
3. Nonviolent Peaceforce: http://nonviolentpeaceforce.org/.
4. Professor Worthington is a leading academic in forgiveness research and
   practice. See Everett L. Worthington Jr., *Forgiveness and Reconciliation:
   Theory and Application* (Oxfordshire, UK: Routledge, Abingdon, 2006).
5. Phil Cousineau, ed., *Beyond Forgiveness: Reflections on Atonement* (San
   Francisco: Jossey-Bass, 2011).
6. Michael A. Singer, *The Untethered Soul: The Journey Beyond Yourself*
   (Oakland, CA: New Harbinger Publications/Noetic Books, 2007).
7. B. Alan Wallace, *The Attention Revolution: Unlocking the Power of the
   Focused Mind* (Boston: Wisdom Publications, 2006).

Chapter 8

1. The World Café can be found at http://www.theworldcafe.com/.
2. The Language of Spirit dialogues can be found at
   http://www.seedgraduateinstitute.org/.
3. David Bohm and F. David Peat, *Science, Order, and Creativity*
   (Oxfordshire, UK: Routledge, 2000).
4. See Johan Galtung, *Peace by Peaceful Means: Peace and Conflict,
   Development and Civilization* (Thousand Oaks, CA: Sage, 1996).
5. J. Kim Wright, *Lawyers as Peacemakers: Practicing Holistic,
   Problem-Solving Law* (Chicago: American Bar Association, 2010).
6. To follow the work of William Ury, visit http://www.williamury.com/.
7. ServiceSpace is at http://www.servicespace.org/.

8. The River Phoenix Center for Peacebuilding has developed an impressive list of programs and services, among them the following: Mediation Services, Peacebuilding 101, Restorative Justice, Nonviolent Communication Skill Building, Peer Mediation for Schools, Peace Leadership Training, Eco-Sustainability, Deep Ecology and Earth Connection, and Men and Women in Healing Dialogue. To find out more, see http://www.centerforpeacebuilding.org/.

Chapter 9

1. To find out more about Avon Mattison's work, see http://www.pathwaystopeace.org/.
2. http://www.vandanashiva.org/.
3. For more on Louise Diamond's work and systems thinking and policy making, see http://www.globalsystemsinitiatives.net/.
4. Don Edward Beck and Christopher C. Cowan, *Spiral Dynamics: Mastering Values, Leadership, and Change* (Malden, MA: Blackwell Publishing, 1996). To follow Don Beck's work, see http://www.spiraldynamics.net/.

Chapter 10

1. See http://www.pachamama.org/.
2. For maps of mind-body wholeness, consult Marilyn Schlitz, Tina Amorok, and Marc Micozzi, *Consciousness and Healing: Integral Approaches to Mind-Body Medicine* (St. Louise: Elsevier, 2004).

Bibliography

Argentine National Commission on the Disappeared. *Nunca Mas: The Report of the Argentine National Commission on the Disappeared.* New York: Farrar Straus & Giroux, 1986.

Arrien, Angeles. *The Four-Fold Way: Walking the Paths of the Warrior, Teacher, Healer, and Visionary.* New York: HarperOne, 1993.

Ausubel, Kenny, and J. P. Harpignies. *Nature's Operating Instructions: The True Biotechnologies (The Bioneers Series).* San Francisco: Sierra Club Books, 2004.

Barash, David P. *The Survival Game: How Game Theory Explains the Biology of Cooperation and Competition.* New York: Holt, 2004.

Baudrillard, Jean, and Marc Guillame. *Radical Alterity.* Translated by Ames Hodges. Los Angeles: Semiotext(e), 2008.

Beck, Don E., and Christopher Cowan. *Spiral Dynamics: Mastering Values, Leadership, and Change.* Hoboken, NJ: Wiley-Blackwell, 2005.

Bennett, J. G. *Gurdjieff: Making a New World.* Santa Fe, NM: Bennett Books, 1992.

Bohm, David, and F. David Peat. *Science, Order, and Creativity.* Oxfordshire, UK: Routledge, 2000.

Capra, Fritjof. *The Hidden Connections: A Science for Sustainable Living.* New York: Vintage/Anchor Books, 2004.

Chopra, Deepak. *Peace Is the Way: Bringing War and Violence to an End.* New York: Three Rivers Press, 2005.

Chopra, Deepak, Debbie Ford, and Marianne Williamson. *The Shadow Effect: Illuminating the Hidden Power of Your True Self.* New York: HarperOne, 2010.

Cousineau, Phil, ed. *Beyond Forgiveness: Reflections on Atonement.* San Francisco: Jossey-Bass, 2011.

De Waal, Frans. *The Age of Empathy: Nature's Lessons for a Kinder Society.* New York: Harmony Books, 2009.

Diamond, Louise. *The Courage for Peace: Daring to Create Harmony in Ourselves and the World.* Berkeley, CA: Conari Press, 2000.

Eisler, Riane, and Ron Miller, eds. *Educating for a Culture of Peace.* Portsmouth, NH: Heinemann, 2004.

Galtung, Johan. *Peace by Peaceful Means: Peace and Conflict, Development and Civilization.* Thousand Oaks, CA: Sage, 1996.

Gerzon, Mark. *Leading through Conflict: How Successful Leaders Transform Differences into Opportunities.* Boston: Harvard Business Review Press, 2006.

Goleman, Daniel. *Emotional Intelligence: 10th Anniversary Edition; Why It Can Matter More Than IQ.* New York: Bantam, 2006.

———. *Social Intelligence: The New Science of Human Relationships.* New York: Bantam Books, 2007.

Houston, Jean. *Manual for the Peacemaker: An Iroquois Legend to Heal Self and Society.* Quest Books, 1995.

Jung, Carl G. *The Portable Jung.* New York: Penguin Books, 1971.

Koestler, Arthur. *The Ghost in the Machine.* New York: Penguin, 1995.

Korten, David C. *The Great Turning: From Empire to Earth Community.* San Francisco: Berrett-Koehler Publishers, 2007.

Koster, Ralph. *A Theory of Fun for Game Design.* Scottsdale, AZ: Paraglyph Press, 2005.

Kuhn, Thomas S. *The Structure of Scientific Revolutions: 50th Anniversary Edition.* Chicago: University of Chicago Press, 2012.

Laszlo, Ervin. *The Chaos Point: The World at the Crossroads.* Newburyport, MA: Hampton Roads Publishing, 2006.

Lederach, John Paul, and Angela Jill Lederach. *When Blood and Bones Cry Out: Journeys through the Soundscape of Healing and Reconciliation.* Queensland, Australia: University of Queensland Press, 2010.

Lipton, Bruce H. *The Biology of Belief: Unleashing the Power of Consciousness, Matter, and Miracles.* 13th ed. Carlsbad, CA: Hay House Books, 2011.

Lipton, Bruce H., and Steve Bhaerman. *Spontaneous Evolution: Our Positive Future and a Way to Get There from Here.* 3rd ed. Carlsbad, CA: Hay House Books, 2010.

Markova, Dawna. *No Enemies Within: A Creative Process for Discovering What's Right About What's Wrong.* Berkeley, CA: Conari Press, 1994.

Merton, Thomas. *Conjectures of a Guilty Bystander.* Image, 1968.

Mitchell, Edgar, with Dwight Williams. *The Way of the Explorer: An Apollo Astronaut's Journey through the Material and Mystical Worlds.* rev. ed. Pompton Plains, NJ: New Page Books, 2008.

O'Dea, James. *Creative Stress: A Path for Evolving Souls Living through Personal and Planetary Upheaval.* Pioneer Imprints, 2010.

Pert, Candace B. *Molecules of Emotion: The Science behind Mind-Body Medicine.* New York: Simon & Schuster, 1999.

Radin, Dean. *Entangled Minds: Extrasensory Experiences in a Quantum Reality.* New York: Paraview Pocket Books, 2006.

Rifkin, Jeremy. *The Empathic Civilization: The Race to Global Consciousness in a World in Crisis.* New York: Jeremy P. Tarcher/Penguin, 2009.

Rosenberg, Marshall. *Nonviolent Communication: A Language of Life.* Encinitas, CA: PuddleDancer Press, 2003.

Scharmer, Otto C. *Theory U: Leading from the Future as It Emerges.* San Francisco: Berrett-Koehler Publishers, 2009.

Senge, Peter M., C. Otto Scharmer, Joseph Jaworski, and Betty Sue Flowers. *Presence: Human Purpose and the Field of the Future.* New York: Crown Business, 2008.

Sharp, Nonie. *No Ordinary Judgment.* Canberra: Aboriginal Studies Press, 1996.

Schlitz, Marilyn, Tina Amorok, and Marc Micozzi. *Consciousness and Healing: Integral Approaches to Mind-Body Medicine.* Philadelphia: Churchill Livingstone/Elsevier, 2004.

Shiva, Vandana. *Earth Democracy: Justice, Sustainability, and Peace.* Brooklyn: South End Press, 2005.

Singer, Michael A. *The Untethered Soul: The Journey Beyond Yourself.* Oakland, CA: New Harbinger Publications/Noetic Books, 2007.

Tutu, Desmond. *No Future without Forgiveness.* Image, 2000.

Ueshiba, Morihei. *The Heart of Aikido: The Philosophy of Takemusu Aiki.* Translated by Moriteru Ueshiba. New York: Kodansha USA, 2010.

Wallace, B. Alan. *The Attention Revolution: Unlocking the Power of the Focused Mind.* Boston: Wisdom Publications, 2006.

Wheatley, Margaret J. *Turning to One Another: Simple Conversations to Restore Hope to the Future.* 2nd ed. San Francisco: Berrett-Koehler Publishers, 2009.

Whitehead, Alfred North. *Science and the Modern World.* New York: Free Press, 1997.

Wilber, Ken. *The Integral Vision: A Very Short Introduction to the Revolutionary Integral Approach to Life, God, the Universe, and Everything.* Boston: Shambhala Publications, 2007.

Wolf, Joachim. *Understanding the Grand Design: Spiritual Reality's Inner Logic.* Bloomington, IN: Trafford Publishing, 2006.

Worthington, Everett L. Jr. *Forgiveness and Reconciliation: Theory and Application.* Oxfordshire, UK: Routledge, Abingdon, 2006.

Wright, J. Kim. *Lawyers as Peacemakers: Practicing Holistic, Problem-Solving Law.* Chicago: American Bar Association, 2010.

Index